D1566939

Womb Prints

2nd Edition

Discover Life's First Impressions

Barbara Findeisen

With a Foreword by Thomas R. Verny

Barbara Findeisen
Email: BFScrabble@me.com

ISBN: 978-1981653393
ISBN: 1981653392

Cataloging-in-Publication Data is on file with the Library of Congress: 2016902769

Cover design by Mike Jones

To My Children
Reid, Mark, and Lisa

And to and my grandchildren
Charlie, Marcus, Joy and Angelina

And to all our children
including the child within each one of us.

Foreword

Since the publication of my book *The Secret Life of the Unborn Child* in 1981, the unborn child's life has become a focus of mass scrutiny, and with each passing year—less secret. Now, Barbara Findeisen has written a book that is an important contribution to the growing canon of research papers and books on this subject.

Womb Prints is based on the author's forty years of work as a licensed psychotherapist with a variety of clients on issues that seemed to originate in their very early experiences either in the womb or shortly after birth. Rather than take the academic route to explore these incidents, Findeisen provides the reader with the actual narratives of her sessions. It is as if you were a fly on the wall of her consulting room, watching and listening as these stories unfold.

Written in jargon-free style, this book is easily accessible to a layperson yet is valuable reading for health professionals. It is not a book that is didactic or preachy, trying to convince or convert. The stories speak for themselves. And they teach us that if we hope to have a better world, we need to start by protecting the amniotic universe of babies from toxins, be they emotional or physical. We do this by love, by taking care of our bodies and our relationships. Children conceived in love, carried for nine months in the mother with love, and born into a loving family will grow up into loving beings.

What these stories tell us is this: Take care of your children from conception on, and they will take good care of you and the planet.

Thomas R. Verny MD, DHL, DPsych, FRCPC, FAPA
Past President APPPAH
Associate Editor, *Journal of Prenatal and Perinatal Psychology and Health*
Author of *The Secret Life of the Unborn Child* (with John Kelly)
and *Pre-Parenting* (with Pamela Weintraub)

Preface

My intention in writing *Womb Prints* is to encourage people to focus their attention on the first human environment—the world of the womb. In those earliest moments, the fetus's brain is already making profound adjustments to adapt to its environment, an environment that will have a lasting impact on the life of the developing individual. What is experienced in that watery world imprints patterns of trust or mistrust, and health or fragility. The world of the womb and the pre- and perinatal time of life contain the roots of optimism and pessimism as well as of love and fear. If we are to have happy, healthy, confident, and compassionate communities, we must pay attention to our children's first impressions in the womb. Survival patterns that begin in the womb are deeply embedded in the developing brain, and they influence the physical, psychological, intellectual, and spiritual aspects of a person's life.

Gestation, birth, early bonding, and attachment experiences are all part of a spectrum that reaches the deepest level of the human psyche. In these most fertile areas, we discover the etiology of a wide range of psychological and behavioral problems. When early experiences are either physically or emotionally traumatic, they leave survival imprints that cast a dysfunctional shadow, lasting in some cases for years until their resolution.

In 2010, the National Institute of Mental Health (NIMH) found that "just over 20 percent (or one in five) children either currently have or, at some point during their life, have had a seriously debilitating mental disorder" (Merikangas et al, 2010). In 2013, the Center for Disease Control and Prevention reported that 13 percent of children ages eight to fifteen had a diagnosable mental disorder the previous year. Attention deficit hyperactivity disorder (ADHD) and posttraumatic stress disorder (PTSD) are now commonly found in children (Centers for Disease Control, n.d.). When we consider all the possible causes of these disorders and of a host of other challenges, our investigation needs to begin in the womb, where the vulnerable brain is developing. This time of a child's earliest and most powerful learning experiences is usually ignored. But today, researchers possess a wealth of information about the emotional and psychological needs of both the unborn and new baby and the lasting effects on the new baby when there is trauma or neglect. This information should not be overlooked.

For those in the medical and mental health fields at all levels, this book is a call to include pre- and perinatal psychology in their medical and mental health practices. For parents, particularly women in the childbearing years, this book is an invitation to see their developing fetuses as conscious, sentient, learning, wondrous creatures who deserve attention and loving care from conception forward.

For people who have already had a child or who are past the childbearing years, this book is a call to reflect on their own early pre- and perinatal experiences and those of their children—without guilt or assigning blame. When I was on the Oprah Winfrey TV show, a woman in the audience angrily called out "Why is it always the mother's fault?" I have heard that question asked many times. The answer is that it isn't always the mother's fault. The majority of women sincerely want to be good mothers. Others, because of physical illness, emotional instability, or circumstances beyond their control, find the task too difficult or impossible. We must remember, too, that all mothers are themselves subject to environments that affect them, including people in those environments who do not realize that to take good care of the mother is to take good care of the future child.

I understand the feeling of guilt. But I urge you to realize that when we carry guilt and blame ourselves, we are attacking ourselves. It serves no good. We did the best we knew. Forgiveness is needed, both of ourselves and of our mothers.

When I gave birth to my three children between 1955 and 1963, I knew nothing about pre- and perinatal psychology. I was raised to do whatever the doctor told me to do. My only personal desire was to have a natural birth. I was not sure what that meant except to be given no drugs. On that one issue, I stood my ground. I wanted to be awake! Otherwise, I did as I was directed. After birth, they took my newborn child away to a nursery and told me I needed to rest and that I would see him in about four hours. I did not protest. It was standard hospital procedure. I was also strongly advised not to nurse my baby because the doctors thought it was better for him and for me to use bottle-feeding, as most of my friends were doing. There are times I still feel the loss of what my babies and I missed—that natural, beautiful time of bonding and attachment. I wish I had known then what I know now.

In the 1960s, there was a lot going on in the San Francisco Bay area where I lived. Even though I was changing diapers and teaching elementary school, I could not ignore the tsunami of New Age consciousness and the revolution that was happening in civil rights and women's rights. Many of my students had emotional problems and learning difficulties, so I searched for ways I could be of more help to them. I knew my best route would be to get more training, so I decided to return to graduate school for a degree in psychology, and I became a licensed therapist.

During this time, I had an experience in therapy that shook my beliefs and changed my life's direction. It made me realize that I had a connection to my life in the womb, and it motivated me to do research and subsequently led me to specialize in pre- and perinatal psychology. The impact of that precise time in my life continues to be validated by the experiences of my clients as well as by the ongoing professional research of others.

Currently, neuroscience and epigenetic research are exploding with information that verifies the extraordinary importance of our earliest experiences and their lasting impact. We know that a fetus is conscious, listening, and responding to the environment of the womb. Before the development of the left brain, the right brain of the fetus is maturing, adjusting, and sensing a flood of new experiences within that environment.

I hope that this book will be read and taken to heart by the broadest possible audience. Equipped with what we know, and with a deep appreciation for the integrity of the soul of every human being, we can change the quality of our lives and that of our children far into the future. How we individually and in community care for our babies and children makes a lasting impact on the future of our society. It is perhaps the single most important way we can touch the future.

Acknowledgements

I have been writing this book for years and have so many individuals to thank that it would take another book to acknowledge all of them. I have much gratitude for their contributions in my life.

My clients—I have learned from and been inspired by each one of you. By working with you, I became a believer in the power of the human spirit.

My colleagues—we have learned and shared with each other, and together we have made a positive difference for so many.

Star Foundation—I am grateful for the Star community, which provided me with years of support and opportunities to do therapeutic work, helping others transform their lives. Thank you for your responsible and marvelous work and for your camaraderie.

Individuals who were mentors to me and who added significantly to the richness of my life and career I would like to mention by name:

Thomas Verny—I will always be grateful to Dr. Verny for his role in founding the Association for Pre- and Perinatal Psychology and Health (APPPAH) and for writing *The Secret Life of the Unborn Child*, the book that validated pre- and perinatal psychology. I will be forever grateful for his wisdom and his friendship.

David Chamberlain—for his years of research and dedication to validating to the world that, indeed, babies are conscious and do remember their births, and for his good humor and advice, my gratitude.

Bruce Lipton—for his groundbreaking work in understanding the biology of love, and for his energetic sharing of cellular biology with such joy and passion, and for his spirit, friendship, and unique ability to always make things fun, I am truly indebted.

Stan Grof—I am grateful for all he has contributed to our understanding of consciousness. With him, I discovered parts of myself previously unknown to me. Stan is a role model for me in his consistent compassion, wisdom, and kindness.

My friends and colleagues in Sweden—I will always be grateful for your support, warm welcome, and love, which made me feel I was part of a Swedish family.

Sandra Verny, Donna Chamberlain, Martha Horton, and all the partners who make it possible for those of us who work tirelessly to carry forward the information of the importance of the entire spectrum of pre- and perinatal psychology, I say bless you, bless you.

My husband, Charlie—I am appreciative and grateful to you for the love and support you gave to me, STAR, and Kenyon Ranch. Without you, it would have been impossible.

My sons, Reid and Mark—thank you for choosing me to be your mother. You and your kids light up my life and bring me joy.

My daughter, Lisa—thank you for all you have taught me.

A special acknowledgement to all the authors whose books have given me so much information and inspiration.

Last but not least, I want to thank Jennifer Newcomb for her patience and dedication to this project as well as her continuous encouragement and hard work. Her compassion and creativity reside in these pages.

The year 2015 saw the passing of three outstanding pioneers in the fields of perinatal and infant care.

Kathryn Barnard, the author of many books, was also an innovator in the care and development of newborns. Recognizing the possible dangers of isolating infants in incubators, she helped invent the Isolette©, which rocks and soothes the baby. The rocking led to faster weight gain and improved motor and sensory functions. She devoted her career to developing programs to improve the mental health of babies. She proved that sensory stimulation and gentle touching helped promote infants' ability to embrace their new world and their place in it. Her work also included research to identify children whose earliest environments placed them at risk.

Elizabeth Bing, who preferred the term "prepared childbirth," sought childbirth alternatives since the late forties and was known as "the mother of Lamaze."

Sheila Kitzinger, the author of numerous books including *Birth Crisis* and *The Complete Book of Pregnancy and Childbirth*, was a strong advocate for women to make informed decisions about their bodies, especially in relation to childbirth.

Personally, and as a community of prenatal psychologists, we deeply miss Dr. David Chamberlain and Joseph Chilton Pearce. Their wisdom and dedication remain as a standard for all of us who care about human life.

Table of Contents

Our birth is but a sleep and a forgetting;
The Soul that rises with us, our life's Star,
    Hath had elsewhere its setting,
    And cometh from afar:
    Not in entire forgetfulness,
    And not in utter nakedness,
But trailing clouds of glory do we come
    From God, who is our home:
Heaven lies about us in our infancy!
Shades of the prison-house begin to close
    Upon the growing Boy,
    But He beholds the light, and whence it flows,
    He sees it in his joy;
The Youth, who daily farther from the east
    Must travel, still is Nature's Priest,
    And by the vision splendid
    Is on his way attended;
At length the Man perceives it die away,
And fade into the light of common day.

WILLIAM WORDSWORTH
"Intimations of Immortality from
Recollections of Early Childhood"

Introduction

In my longtime career as a therapist, my clients have been my greatest teachers. It has been quite an education. Perhaps the greatest lesson I have learned is how to listen. Listening is not the same as hearing. The late French otolaryngologist Alfred Tomatis (1988/2005) described hearing as being passive, but in listening, the whole body reaches out, and the individual becomes an "antenna." Children know the difference and stop communicating if they are only being heard, not listened to. Babies will also feel the difference.

Early in my practice, I began to see the difference between doing and being. I remember a businessman named Clark who made an appointment to see me. I was in Europe to speak at a professional conference, and at such conferences it was not unusual for individuals to book one or two sessions with me. This handsome, impeccably dressed gentleman was about forty. At first, we talked about what he hoped to accomplish in his session. He said he wanted to regress back to a significant event in his lifetime; he hoped it would explain why he had certain feelings. At this point in time, regression therapy was somewhat new to me, and I was refining how to listen and be open to the outcome. Another important lesson I was learning was that though I was in charge of the session, I was not in control of the process. These lessons were reinforced by my work with Clark.

I guided him into a deep state of relaxation until I sensed he was in peaceful place. I sat quietly. After five to ten minutes, I began to get restless and prayed for guidance. I heard a voice within telling me to "do nothing." After more time passed, I again became anxious. I heard my Yankee mother's puritan work ethic saying, "He's paying you! Do something." Then I heard the earlier voice with a stronger, rather curt message to "shut up." Not exactly the voice of the spirit, but I obeyed. This pattern continued for almost two hours.

Eventually, Clark began to stir, and his eyes blinked opened. He turned his head and looked at me very intently, and then he quietly said, "Thank God you didn't say anything." He went on to tell me about being in a sacred place of peace and beauty where he listened to celestial music and received profound insights and guidance concerning his life. As I listened to him, I felt grateful I had heeded the inner voice that knew my silence was essential to his experience.

What I did not expect when I became a therapist was that I would be witness to so many spiritual transformations. It appears that when individuals have the courage to confront their deepest fears and pain, they find more than skeletons from their past. They also find the gold of their souls, or their "soul child." This special being, depicted in literature, fairy tales, myths, and religious texts, sees reality through the heart of a wise, compassionate being and speaks the language of mystics, ancient prophets, and modern sages. Clients often stumble upon their soul child when they revisit the beginnings of their lives, for they frequently lost it there.

Accompanied by feelings of profound love, the discovery of the soul child during therapy often leaves clients dumbfounded by their own testimony, which reflects the perennial wisdom of the ages. They become aware of the spirit within them. In reflecting on a regression session, sudden epiphanies or healing insights occur. In the process, rich layers of meaning are added to their personal stories.

The stories in *Womb Prints* shine a spotlight on pre- and perinatal issues involving pain and violence as well as joy and love. Each story is unique, yet in each there is a common thread. We all know the feelings of sadness, fear, anger, and pain. We also know the feelings of warmth, joy, and love. We can relate to one another's stories. In the nonjudgmental company of others, our hearts open up and discover our true natures. We see the paths that we walked and, in the process, we find meaning and purpose.

It is my hope that in reading the stories in *Womb Prints*, you will find yourself and your heart will open, and you will share your stories. As my friend Louis Herman wrote in *Future Primal* (2013), "Ultimately, since all our knowing is inevitably refracted by our own unique trajectory through life, all we have to teach is contained within our own story."

Therapy not only gives us an opportunity to tell our stories but also can provide a new way of seeing. With a map to follow, we not only discover our authenticity, we find each other. In the telling and the listening, a sacred space is created, and in this space, the past and present come together in the service of the future. As Wordsworth (1807) so elegantly said, "The soul rises with us, our life's Star."

1

Echoes from the Womb:
Stories of Positive Womb Experiences

Each second we live is a new and unique moment of the universe, a moment that will never be again. And what do we teach our children?...
We should say to each of them: Do you know what you are? You are a marvel. You are unique. In all the years that have passed, there has never been another child like you. Your legs, your arms, your clever fingers, the way you move...You have the capacity for anything. Yes, you are a marvel. And when you grow up, can you harm another who is, like you, a marvel? You must work, we must all work to make the world worthy of its children.

PABLO CASALS

We learn our first lessons in the watery world of the womb. Therein lies the exquisite sensitivity and awareness of the infant before birth. If we feel loved and welcomed in the womb, we know who we are, and we know we belong. If we feel unwelcomed and threatened in the womb, we do not feel safe or that we belong. One lesson is a blessing. The other lesson is a challenge.

Those lessons stay with us. In Lloyd de Mause's (1982) words,

Mental life begins in the womb in a fetal drama, which is remembered and elaborated upon by later childhood events. Patterns are actually imposed on the musculature and then on the cortex itself, as imprints or memories, which remain like a permanent "motion picture" to influence our conscious and future reactions (p.244).

When a dangerous environment is present in the womb, fear grows and along with it a compulsive need to be on guard. This can be seen years later in adults who live as chronic pessimists. Self-talk and behaviors reflect that position. So does the body, with tension and the inability to relax. These individuals are unable to trust and believe that they can find happiness.

When Louis Pasteur lay dying and was reflecting on his most famous theory, he admitted in the presence of his lifetime adversary on germ cell theory, scientist Claude Bernard, that Bernard was right: "The seed is nothing, the soil is everything" (Middleton, 2009, p.1) A seedling planted in a salty environment or a seedling assaulted by chemicals may not survive, or it may survive as a stunted version of its potential. For human babies, the soil is the environment of the mother. Of course, mothers may be subject to a larger environment over which they have little control: the quality of a mother's relationship with the father, the support (or lack thereof) by her immediate communities, prevailing wars, poverty, hunger, and other deprivations can be powerful influences. It is staggering to contemplate the future of children carried and birthed by mothers who exist in current international crises.

Because of the significance of life before birth and the powerful influence the womb environment has on brain development, life in the womb may be the most important period in an individual's history. Seeds of optimism or pessimism are planted very early as the brain is developing and the fetus is responding both physically and emotionally to the state of the mother. David Chamberlain describes this natural process in *Windows to the Womb: Revealing the Conscious Baby from Conception to Birth*: "In the earliest experiences in the womb, babies need no instructions to grasp the emotional tones of the transactions that are unfolding" (Chamberlain, 2013, p.118).

Traditional and Contemporary Wisdom

Knowledge about the influence of the womb on the unborn child has been grounded in traditions before it was verified by research. In ancient China, the pregnant mother was encouraged to think only peaceful thoughts and surround herself with beauty to avoid evil spirits. Other ancient and indigenous societies have long accepted that the emotional well-being of a pregnant woman influences, both negatively and positively, the future well-being of her child. A dear Greek friend of mine spoke to me on more than one occasion of the practice in ancient Greece whereby special quarters and gardens, abundant in art and beauty, were reserved for pregnant women. Indeed, traditions that include special attention and practices for the mother and child often go beyond the parameters of the pregnancy.

The modern world often views such traditional wisdom as superstition, and some of it may be, though anecdotal data proves that prenatal influences can "mark" a child. One such anecdote comes from the biography of Frank Lloyd Wright. Wright's mother was said to have declared the child she was carrying would grow up to build beautiful buildings. To cultivate his awareness, she decorated his nursery with engravings of English cathedrals she had taken out of a periodical (Secrest, 1992, p.72). A trained teacher, she also purchased educational blocks (created by Friedrich Wilhelm Froebel in 1876), which Wright cited in his autobiography as influential in his approach to design: "For several years I sat at the little Kindergarten tabletop…and played…with the cube, the sphere and the triangle—these smooth wooden maple blocks…All are in my fingers to this day" (Wright, 1943, p.51).

British-American anthropologist and author Ashley Montague stated that the infant is learning what to expect in life even before his birth: "Important potentials for conditioning and probably learning are already present in the unborn fetus, as well as the possibility of acquiring certain habits of response while still in the womb" (Montagu, 1962, p.433). Recent research has shown that maternal anxiety has an effect on neonatal motor activity (for example, irregularity of biological functions) and later on infant behavior and temperament (for example, crying activity and aggressiveness). Van der Bergh and Marceon (2004) studied eight- and nine-year-old children who had experienced prenatal stress and found that

> maternal anxiety during pregnancy seems to influence postnatal behaviors and temperamental dispositions of the child, which imply self-regulatory mechanisms and resiliency. In boys, prenatal anxiety had a clear effect on inhibitory control, hyperactivity, attention disorders and aggression. Girls showed more social problems and externalizing behaviors (p.1092).

Referring to a study of 7,477 women and their children by O'Connor, Heron, Golding and Glover, Van der Bergh (2004) noted that

> ... preliminary evidence suggests that antenatal maternal activity is indeed a real and specific risk factor for behavioral problems in the child such as hyperactivity, inattention and emotional problems in boys and conduct disorders in girls (p.1096).

Experience Influences Perception

If, as some philosophers and mystics claim, we are responsible for the world we see, our "seeing" is colored by what we have experienced. Gerald Huther, author of *The Compassionate Brain*, described this process:

Those neuronal networks and synaptic pathways that have been stabilized by virtue of repeated early experiences tend to become permanent; the synapses that are not used often enough tend to be eliminated. In this way early experiences—positive or negative—have a decisive impact on how the brain is wired. ...Insecurely attached children have difficulties to acquire a broad spectrum of different coping strategies, to maintain a high level of creativity and curiosity, to constructively interact with others, and to develop feelings of connectedness, love and peace (Huther, 2013, p.30).

Deeply imprinted early trauma leads to a sense of helplessness for the victim, who learns to perceive the world as a pessimist. He sees everything that is "wrong" or worries about what could go wrong, and then lives in the reality of his perception. He sees a catastrophe and dramatizes.

Martin Seligman, in *Learned Optimism*, cited three attributes to the learned helplessness of the pessimist: "permanence, personalization, and pervasiveness" (Seligman, 1991, p.45). The pessimist feels as if the situation is hopeless and will always remain so. He interprets events with very little faith that life could be different. Sometimes his perception becomes an ingrained belief he defends as being right, even if he is proven wrong. He attracts rejection and punishment, which becomes a self-c fulfilling prophecy.

In contrast, the optimist looks through a different lens and expects good things to happen. The optimist is hopeful and better able to "go with the flow." The optimist attracts support and affirmation, which serves to reinforce success. Like Forrest Gump a character in the movie by that name, the optimist says "Shit happens," but he doesn't allow it to get him down.

Unfortunately, there are children and adults who are locked into a chronic stress response from as early as the womb and birth. Nervous, frightened mothers tend to produce fear-based babies who have difficulty relaxing. Pessimism becomes a defense, and it is defended. The baby mirrors the mother's responses.

When a pregnancy is strongly unwanted, the baby begins life's journey with a handicap, as uterine conditions for an unwanted fetus do not support a positive primary prenatal connection with the mother. When this first relationship is fragmented or shattered, the child's ability to form strong, loving relationships later may be compromised.

Evidence suggests that early rejection may play a role in premature births, difficulties in the birthing process, breastfeeding, and secure attachment. Levend and Janus have reported that the interplay between being unwanted and of violence during pregnancy forms a significant background for later dis-sociability and a tendency towards committing violent crimes (Levand & Janus, 2000).

In extreme cases such as violent rape or incest, the mother may hate the fetus. The fetus is seen as being connected to the abuser and is an unwanted and painful memory, a continual reminder of the trauma. The energy of the mother's anger infiltrates the womb environment. Though there are exceptions, the offspring may not experience any positive prenatal bonding. Consequently, patterns are set for later emotional and behavioral problems. Gestating in a rejecting, angry womb may result in a later desire for revenge. I have written in the past of clients calling their hearts "hardened" or "closed." I have also described babies born in an alert state of hypervigilance, never having felt safe or welcomed. From such hardened hearts, we can hardly expect compassion and peace to flow.

Without help, these deeply wounded fetuses may become difficult children or teenagers who act out. They may become adults who at one end of a continuum are codependent, unable to relax or connect meaningfully to others, as they are always trying to find someone to fill their bottomless cup of need. At the other end of the continuum, they may become criminals, murderers, rapists, abusers, or addicts, smoldering with rage. Underneath their behavior, they are terrified and hide their helplessness and grief. They actually yearn for love and intimate connections, which they simultaneously unconsciously fear. They fill the hole in their hearts with revenge and create their horror. They dare not be vulnerable. Ultimately, they hide their souls from themselves and everyone else.

Positive Womb Experiences

Working in pre- and perinatal psychology, I have had the opportunity to witness both negative and positive womb influences. Babies who have been cared for and loved prenatally have a base of expecting love. They are therefore more responsive, trusting, and easier to love than crying, resistant infants with "problems," who may not like to be touched or cuddled. Whether positive or negative, such patterns become habituated and extend into adulthood and can even perpetuate into the next generation.

Research shows that positive interactions lead to an easier and faster development of cognitive and emotional skills. Thomas Verny writes, "Such interactions confer not just temporary advantages, but permanent ones because they are evolution's number one tool for constructing the brain" (Verny & Weintaub, 2002, p.8). This construction begins prenatally and continues after birth. It is the soil nourishing the roots of who we become.

I want to speak now of my observations of those blessed by a good womb of uterine bliss. Here are two stories of individuals who experienced the loving world of a secure attachment.

Victor

Victor shared how much he felt loved by his mother in the womb. He told me, "I was born with that gift, with the memory that magic exists. I remember that was my mother's intention. It wasn't just to have me, but to have me so I could experience something beyond. That was her clear intention."

Even though he was separated temporarily from her after he was born, he retained the goodness from the original environment provided for him during gestation. He spoke of the loving ways his parents interacted with him, and how he intuitively understood their genuine, positive spiritual connection.

From my years of listening and observing, I have noticed that young children, even infants, have an innate sense of spirituality and altruism. Later, this largesse may fade or be ridiculed by "bigger" people, since we are often conditioned to dismiss or deny that spiritual presence. This reductive transformation is what one of my clients referred to when he said, "I am beginning to forget." But Victor's parents reinforced and supported his connection to spirit in their relationships with him, in spite of the difficult realities of their lives. Victor remembered that experience: "The truth is, when they did interact with me, it was very, very positive. I had that in the womb."

This positive experience remained with him and left him with optimism, in spite of his challenging daily reality. Victor did not have a safe environment when he was growing up in Harlem, witnessing gunfights and murders on the street outside his window. He lived in cramped quarters with his grandparents and dysfunctional family members, including an aunt who was schizophrenic. To make ends meet, his parents lived and worked in another small town and came home on weekends. Victor grew up in a chaotic, unsafe apartment in a crime-ridden neighborhood. But his original imprint in the womb was so strong that, as he observed to me, "the inner core kept me going throughout—why else would I have turned out all right, given the neighborhood and the poverty I lived in?"

As a child, he instinctively sought out individuals who reinforced that positive core. He found them among nuns, his Jesuit teachers, and later among professors at Harvard. He attracted compassionate and wise people into his life. Just as individuals who have experienced toxic wombs or early trauma are on guard while they look for trouble or seem to be almost a magnet for negativity, Victor, with his early positive imprinting, seemed to anticipate and attract the best offerings of the world. He was very different from Forrest Gump, but both were optimists. The script was the same, though the participants and sets were different.

Perhaps the greatest blessing a mother can bestow on her child is a healthy and loving beginning within the safe, warm world of her body. Victor received such a gift from his mother. The soil in which Victor was planted enriched him and guided him to seek what was good. His story illustrates just how valuable a good womb can be throughout one's life. He first learned what to expect based on the environment provided by his parents. His was an imprint to expect support and love. He kept "the magic," and it has continuously blessed his life.

Sam

At the suggestion of a friend, Sam came to one of my residential STAR therapy groups. He was a dynamic businessman in his sixties, divorced, with two grown children. His life was good: he had his family, friends, financial success, and faith. There was no crisis or any particular problems in his life at the time.

One day during a guided meditation, an image flashed into his mind of being a baby in a pram, looking up at a tree covered with vibrant yellow flowers. Being from California, I thought it might be an acacia tree in bloom. He smiled as he thought about the memory of his mother and grandmother sitting nearby while they enjoyed a beautiful sunny day. He felt their warm, loving glow around him as he described the moment.

Later, he told me about his birth. He reported that he had heard the story many times. He had been born at his home in Budapest with a doctor in attendance and in the presence of his grandmother and father. He had nursed at his mother's breast, and he had been held, cuddled, and kissed by the proud and delighted family. He abided in all the hallmarks of bonding.

When he later regressed to his birth, his body relaxed, and he drifted into a peaceful reverie. He again felt the warm glow around him and the love and ecstatic joy of the four adults. He heard soft, soothing sounds and felt completely safe. He knew with every fiber of his being that he was cherished, wanted, and exactly where he belonged and wanted to be. In the words of attachment theory, he was securely attached.

A few days later in another session, he had a totally different experience. He saw himself as a five-year-old boy, sloshing knee- deep in mud. The only thing that was the same was the presence of his father, mother, and grandmother. Everything else was frightening. It was bitter cold, and they were weary. He saw fear and concern in his family's faces.

They were marching with many others who also appeared to be worried and afraid.

When soldiers with guns began shouting and guard dogs began barking incessantly, the march became chaotic and noisy. Sam's mother gripped his hand even tighter. The soldiers herded and shoved people into lines and then sent the queues in different directions. For some unknown reason, all four members of his family were directed to the same place. Sam was very happy and relieved about this. Everything else seemed scary, but his family was with him.

Sam's story is about going from a safe, loving home to a Nazi concentration camp. It dramatically confirms the power of love in the face of extreme evil.

At the camp, the grown-ups worked while Sam spent the days with the other children; all of them were anxious and fearful of the evil that surrounded them. Life was not as it used to be. Everyone was hungry and struggling to stay alive. His parents tried to keep some semblance of their family life. Sam could still recall the look on his mother's face as she lighted whatever candles she could scrounge for Friday Seder. In the flickering candlelight, even in this most miserable of places, he saw the look of love on her face. He never forgot it. Years later, whenever there were challenges, he remembered that look on his mother's face in the glow of the candles.

Occasionally, his father would go out into the night and walk along the perimeter of the encampment. One evening, he noticed another man, a farmer, also out walking, only on the opposite side of the barbed-wire fence. As the days progressed, the two men passed one another several more times. Eventually, they spoke briefly in whispers. They chanced speaking German and were glad they found a tongue in common. Carefully and slowly, Sam's father and the farmer developed a tentative friendship, even though it was totally forbidden. They met in the quiet of the night hours, and sometimes the farmer brought a hunk of bread or a much-treasured piece of cheese that he would slip through the fence to the prisoner. Sam told me how his mother would separate every piece of food she received into ten pieces, one for each family member, and the remaining six pieces for others nearby.

During one chance meeting between the father and the farmer, who turned out to be Ukrainian, the farmer asked, "Do you know why you are here?" Sam's father replied, "Yes, to work." Shaking his head from left to right, the farmer said, "No, to die. I don't want that to happen to you."

Sometime later, when the two men again crossed paths, the fence between them, the farmer whispered that he had a plan to save the small family. He asked the Jewish father to bring his family to a certain place along the edge of the camp on a specific night when there would be no moon.

The family did as he asked. At the meeting place, they silently crawled through the hole the farmer had cut in the fence and followed him away from the camp to a small farm. He led them through the dark night and guided them to their next stop. He had dug out a makeshift cave underneath the chicken coop, where the Nazi patrols and their dogs would only encounter the rank smell of chickens and the family could remain undetected. Sam was taken into the house. He was to act as though he were the farmer's nephew who was sent away from the city to be safe in the country on his uncle's farm. Sam was instructed to never speak a word of German to anyone and to never wander off. At the kind hand of a stranger, Sam's family was able to escape from the concentration camp.

As the war ground on, the fortunes of the family's enemies gradually began to change. The resistance effort would need to continue their press before the allied forces finally got the upper hand. The family of four, three hidden in a hollow under the chicken coop and their son disguised in the house of a stranger, all survived the camp, yet they knew they must continue their journey through the dangerous landscape of war. One night, they were once again rescued, this time by partisans. Following the example of their rescuers, Sam, his grandmother, and his parents hid in the day and walked at night, scavenging whatever food they could find.

During those terrible times, there were many unreported humanitarian acts of kindness—courageous acts by ordinary people who weren't seeking any reward. Like the farmer, his wife, and the partisans, people helped simply because it was the right and compassionate thing to do.

After the war ended, the family was finally able to find their way back to Budapest, only to discover that their home was in a shambles and there was no welcome for them. They decided to walk to Rome, where it was rumored they could find help. Once there, they lined up with many other people and patiently waited for a meal offered by the Salvation Army. Sam paused in the telling of his story to tell me that ever since that time, he has donated to the Salvation Army every year. Eventually, Sam's grandmother was able to get passage to Israel. He and his parents went to Canada.

I found myself wondering what kind of woman his mother must have been. What kind of compassion and faith motivated her to divide precious food so that as many as possible could eat?

How did she manage to honor the Sabbath of her faith in such bleak circumstances? Was she an optimist regardless of the atrocities she had witnessed in a death camp? What was it that empowered her and her family to survive, and beyond even that, to later thrive in a new land with a new culture and a new language?

Everyone who reads Sam's story will have a personal slant on it or assign a different meaning or explanation to it. I would take my stand with the words of Bessel van der Kolk: "Children whose parents are reliable sources of comfort and strength have a lifetime advantage—a kind of buffer against the worst that fate can hand them."[14]

Summing Up

We know that both good wombs and toxic wombs influence brain development and have lasting effects. The presence of love and safety leaves patterns of trust, whereas prenatal trauma leaves patterns of resistance and fear. Negative conditioning and trauma dull or destroy the place of compassion and peace in the brain.

It is not surprising, therefore, that my therapy work suggests that the prenatal environment can affect the well-being of individuals who are adopted after birth. The research I have done indicates that even given the trauma of relinquishment, babies who had a nurturing womb environment seem to do better with accepting their new parents and adapting to new challenges. In contrast, infants who had toxic or frightening prenatal experiences are tenser, less trusting, and as a result, may find adapting to their adoption difficult. As anxious babies, they are more vulnerable to changes and less responsive. They are in greater danger of developing problems with attachment, which is the logical progression of prenatal rejection and fear. Birth, after all, is not a beginning, but a continuation.

The world we first experience is the one we project onto the world. Fortunately, the effect of negative prenatal experiences can be changed by consistent experiences of love.

2

Second Nature:
Adapting to the Womb

Imitation is our most fundamental social skill.
It assures that we automatically pick up and reflect the behavior of our
parents, teachers and peers.

BESSEL VAN DER KOLK

As with all mammals, Nature has designed it so a baby will recognize the very source of his life, survival, and safety—his mother. Her face, touch, smell, and voice are all things he becomes accustomed to; in effect, she and her way of relating to him become his "second nature," a kind of second skin. She is the first one to imprint the developing infant, and adapting to her is for the infant a survival mechanism.

Prenatally, the infant's world is his mother's world. If she is stressed, he becomes stressed. When she is relaxed, he relaxes. Her experiences become his experiences. In the words of Ashley Montagu, "What the infant wants is a womb with a view" (Montagu, 1989, p.62). The mother provides that window. If she sees life through the eyes of fear, her biology will respond with stress hormones. If she sees her surroundings as supportive and loving, her biology will respond with the hormones of love and security. Either will be communicated to the developing fetus.

After birth, the mother's modeling continues to serve as a template that will influence the infant's interpretation of, and responses to, later conditions and events. Babies mirror their models and reflect what they see, and growing children mirror their models and reflect what they see. Parents condition their children just as they were conditioned. In the process, our second nature becomes habituated, and in time, it feels like who we are.

If the infant's environment is toxic and dangerous, the conditioning received from the parents and the environment overpowers the original, essential self and leads to the development of an inauthentic self. As aptly observed by A. R. Raffi, "The psychopathology of the mother is reflected in the child and in later development it appears as his own" (Raffi, 2000, p.30.) Eventually, we believe our adaptations and false identities are true. Yet there is always some degree of anxiety in not feeling "real" because the false identity is merely an act we must continue to reaffirm and make real.

In Jung's terminology, when a person experiences repetitive severe trauma, the false self may split into multiple personas, or the repeated trauma may lead to serious pathology, withdrawal, violence, or even a loss of the soul. If the outcome is not physical death, it can be a psychological death, often accompanied by a yearning to be "invisible." Individuals who have experienced severe trauma and toxic environments often come into therapy feeling they want a "new skin," or to be born again.

In therapy, they find a way to repair early damage and transform the habits of second nature, as the following stories show.

Kate

One day a client named Kate came to my office complaining of a pattern that troubled her. She would compulsively withdraw her energy from any project just as it was about to be successful. She felt she would be "too much" if she ever allowed herself to really let go and succeed. As a child, she had lived on the edge of her family and friends, and as an adult, she always held herself back. She felt unwilling to commit to anything or anybody.

We traced her feelings back to several specific events in her childhood that had caused her to feel she was "too much." In another session, as Kate relaxed into the memories of her past, her mood turned. She felt she was in her mother's womb. She curled up in a fetal position and began to rock back and forth. She said her mother was screaming "This baby is too much for me. I can't handle her. She's too big—it will kill me." Kate's hands went to her heart as she said, "Oh, my heart hurts so much. I must make my heart small. It is the only part of me I can make small."

As a baby, Kate had internalized that she was the "it" her mother thought would kill her. The imprint stayed with her at an unconscious level. Even if she did not understand the words, she felt the energy. The unconscious message stopped her from fulfilling her potential. She had been "shrinking" her heart. This not only affected what she was striving to accomplish, but all her relationships as well. She remained on guard lest she be "too much" for her mother and "kill" her.

Phyllis

Phyllis gestated in the terrifying womb of a schizophrenic mother. It was a dangerous world for both mother and baby. Her mother had become hysterical when she realized that she was pregnant, and Phyllis had "heard" her screaming, "My God, why are you punishing me? My God, why are you punishing me?"

Phyllis was in a deep trance when she re-experienced her birth. She whispered to me, "When I heard her say that, my heart dried up like an old black chicken heart. I wish they'd take me and just put me in a jar of formaldehyde and leave me on the shelf."

Phyllis's type of imprint left her with an unconscious death wish: to her, death seemed like a release. This type of imprint is not uncommon in people with a history of severe trauma. If their original trauma is triggered and they feel the situation is hopeless, they see suicide as a release—not just a way to the end their pain, but their only way out.

Phyllis went to school, married, and was always trying to appear "normal." She trained herself to fit in, to always be agreeable, and to do the right thing. She hardened her heart and relied heavily on her intellect to function in the world. She never got angry and was never spontaneous and playful. Instead, she maintained an identity that was careful and appropriate. She had no children and did not want any. She said she felt they were "messy and unpredictable." Perhaps at an unconscious level, she implicitly knew she would not be able to love them, just as her mother had been unable to love her.

Ellen

When Ellen came to me for therapy, she told me she had dealt with years of chronic depression accompanied by a yearning to escape. Escape from what, or from whom? These feelings had been a part of her for as long as she could remember. As often as Ellen dreamed of freedom, she doubted it could ever be true for her. Her depression had become second nature to her, as if it existed within each breath.

In many sessions, she struggled with sad memories of her childhood, especially the time she spent with her mother, who had been diagnosed as manic-depressive, now referred to as bipolar. Suffering from dramatic mood swings, from deep suicidal depression to excited highs, even sleepless states, Ellen's mother had become pregnant when her husband was in the service, and she was not happy about it. She was not allowed to travel with her husband to various army posts because she had to stay home with her mother-in-law. The pregnancy was not fun, and she resented being trapped. This was not a happy time for her or Ellen. Ellen said, "I remember the feeling that she did not want me, and being overwhelmed by her negative feelings. It was the first time in my life I wanted to die."

Ellen's prenatal environment was filled with the chemistry of her mother's depression and fears alternating with the rush of her mother's adrenaline highs. After her birth regression, Ellen reported, "I felt desperate to get out. I wanted to take off my clothes. I wanted to take off my skin. I could taste the ether. I felt truly overwhelmed by being in the womb and feeling all of my mother's feelings."

In the womb, Ellen had learned to mirror her mother's feelings, to be like her mother. These feelings had become her adaptive second nature. Lacking cognitive skills and understanding, and living under the skin of her mother, she was vulnerable to the contents of her mother's unconscious, which formed the patterns of her own lifelong depression.

However, she also wanted to get away from the toxic negativity of her mother's emotional state. The feelings she had of wanting to "get out of her body, to die" accurately reflected her desire as an infant in her mother's womb to get out of her mother's body.

Later in life, she had suicidal emotions of "wanting to get out of her body, to die." She still carried around with her the feelings of wanting to get out of her mother's body. In therapy, she realized that it was not her own body but her mother's pain from which she wanted to free herself. It was transforming to realize the difference. Psychologically, Ellen had never freed herself.

To claim her authentic self, she made a courageous choice to take the therapeutic journey. Ellen's brother chose another path. Caught in psychosis and unresolved long-term pain, he died during a murderous, psychotic episode. Ellen was more fortunate. Toward the end of her mother's life, she took care of her mother and began to see her mother in a different light. Having healed early wounds and relinquished old perceptions, she and her mother were finally able to find the love they had missed. Amends were made. Ellen said, "She and I truly fell in love with each other in the end." Ellen is now writing a book about honoring parents. Second nature has given way to a rebirth of first nature.

Sharon

Like Ellen, Sharon came into therapy because she suffered from chronic depression. Traditional therapy and medications had helped, but her morning depressions continued. She reported waking up every morning with a dreadful feeling of hopelessness and despair. She hoped regression therapy might give her the healing she had sought for years.

In one of her sessions, Sharon regressed to an embryonic state very early in her life. Breathing evenly and deeply, she seemed without any tension. A faint smile appeared. She described her experience as a fetus later with these words: "I was out in the universe. I was full of awe, wonder, and curiosity. I wanted to come to earth, and be with people. I loved being in the womb. I felt so at home and so connected." This was a deeply moving experience for Sharon; it opened her emotionally and connected her to her spirit.

A few minutes after I saw the faint smile on Sharon's face while she was still in a regressed state, I made the suggestion that she move ahead to the time her mother first became aware of Sharon's presence. Sharon frowned, her body became rigid, and her breathing became shallow and labored. She whispered, "I am freezing in fear. I have to protect my mother and myself. I must not cause a disturbance."

Whatever her mother was experiencing froze Sharon into a stance of vigilance and protection, which was to become a prominent theme throughout Sharon's life and would remain a controlling factor in how she lived. Sharon spoke of the heaviness and familiarity of that emotional state. Though she dreaded waking to the heavy depression she felt each morning, she had come to expect it as "my cross to bear."

Sharon's mother had been kind to her, and there had never been any traumas in Sharon's childhood that explained her fear or her depression. For those reasons, Sharon had a difficult time accepting the power of the shock she had experienced in the regression and the extent to which the early imprint had colored her life.

In a quest for understanding, after she completed STAR, Sharon visited her ninety-year-old mother and asked about her birth. Her mother said, "Well dear, we were so thrilled we were going to have a girl after having three boys. It was a wonderful pregnancy." But Sharon realized that fifty years ago, there was no valid way of knowing a baby's sex before birth. Her mother could not have known she was carrying a baby girl.

In further questioning, her mother identified Sharon's "prenatal shock." The doctor had warned Sharon's mother against having another baby, saying, "Carrying another child may kill you!" When her mother discovered she was pregnant again, she panicked. As a fetus, Sharon must have received that jolt of stress hormones and contracted in fear.

Her parents chose to continue the pregnancy, hoping they might be blessed with a little girl. But throughout that time, they were constantly worried and fearful. Their anxieties became an ongoing part of the environment in which Sharon was developing. Sharon took on those anxieties. She later wore that heavy emotional cloak for fifty years as if it were part of her nature.

In spite of her depression, Sharon had always been "very good" and had never caused a disturbance. Her angst and sense of separation were kept deep within. Others saw her as a perfect role model as a wife and mother. She adapted and became the person she was expected to be. In the bargain, she lost her feelings of awe, wonder, and curiosity.

Unfortunately, no one had ever guessed the root of her problem began in her mother's womb. The depression Sharon's mother felt vanished the moment she saw her beautiful baby girl and knew they were both safe. Her mother had been thrilled! It was not so easy for the infant. Research confirms the baby may carry negative emotions long after the mother has released them. Sharon had accepted depression and the need to be contained as part of her second nature. These feelings had been part of "her world." She had emerged from the womb, but the fears and tension came with her. She remained on guard.

Understanding the source of her chronic depression lifted it from her. In an amazing moment of insight, she said, "Those are her feelings. Not mine! I don't have to keep her feelings."

Now, after therapy at STAR, Sharon was waking up in the morning to a much brighter world. Finally, she could leave her fears and tension behind for good. She could see how pervasive her early adaptation had been in her life, and she realized that she had parented her sons in the same way she had been parented. She had taken excellent care of them, but she had been unable to nurture them emotionally. She said, "I didn't know what that was."

Healing very early pre- and perinatal wounds opened Sharon's heart, making it easier for her to love and be loved. She told me, "I now have experienced love, what it is like to truly love other people. It is a very strong feeling within me now." Loving is not just about doing the right thing for others. Loving is a matter of the heart, a feeling. This was a reflection of Sharon's first nature, which could be said to be love.

Bruce

Bruce's first lessons were of shame and guilt, absorbed from his mother when he was in her womb. She had gotten pregnant "out of wedlock," which in a small southern town was considered a grievous mistake if not a "downright sin." Reluctantly, his father had agreed to "do the right thing" and marry the young mother. Then, throughout Bruce's childhood, he routinely beat both Bruce and his mother. To the outside world, they presented a happy, church-going family, but behind closed doors, it was anything but. Bruce told me,

> He beat the shit out of her or out of me. He beat her all the time. I realized this fear and anxiety I felt all my life started in the womb. My father felt the way he did about me because of the situation surrounding my mother's pregnancy.

At his birth, Bruce remembers screaming, "I am here! I am here!" But the world outside didn't have any time to stop and think about him. There was no warm welcome, no kind thought for this baby.

I saw that one of the reasons he treated me so poorly, abused me, and neglected me, and did the same with my mother, was that he thought he'd done her a real favor. To keep me from being a child of an unwed mother, he married her. Once the wedding was over, he felt he didn't owe us anything else. In fact, he had earned a license to dump his anger on us.

The beatings by his father, and the abuse he saw his mother receive, reinforced Bruce's inner anxiety and lack of self-esteem. Once, when he was almost a full-grown man but still a teenager, he confronted his father and stopped him from beating his mother. Bruce said, "He never beat me again. I used to beg my mother to leave him. I guess she felt she had to stay with him because he had married her."

Being an intelligent and industrious boy, he did well in school and worked at odd jobs to have his own spending money. He also ran away from home several times and stayed away for months at a time before returning. He learned to survive on his own. But whenever he left, he carried what he had accepted and learned to expect along with him.

After high school and college, he graduated from law school and became a successful attorney. However, his inner life remained shaky. Relationships were difficult for him to maintain. With depression and anxiety licking his boots, he escaped into his work. When he came to STAR, he had been involved in therapy and recovery for several years. He was keenly aware of the impact his father had had on his inner instability and chronic level of anxiety.

In exploring his early life in the womb, he experienced surprising revelations.

I was obviously unplanned. There was some kind of secret wedding. I could feel the fear my mother had when she had to tell my father that she was pregnant. I could feel the anger and the frustration of not being wanted . . .

After the birth regression, I put a lot of things together. I began to understand and feel myself as a separate spiritual being from my parents. I may have shared their DNA, but I'm me.

It was a statement of his inherent right to acknowledge all the wondrous aspects of his being and to be himself. This is not a statement to be taken lightly! Bruce was discovering his first nature, the self he had forgotten, his unique "something spiritual. I'm me! I'm not just their mistake."

Many of the pieces of the puzzle of his life began to fall into place, bringing relief and some sense of healing.

In the regression, I started at some place other than the womb— before. The feeling I got was absolutely crystal clear that I'm not just their son. I don't owe them my life. I'm something from beyond. I'm not just their mistake.

When he recognized this unconscious judgment ("just their mistake") and realized it had influenced his entire life, he was able to lift the burden of guilt and shame from his mind. Most assuredly, in the womb he had absorbed his mother's strong feelings of guilt, shame, and fear. The years of abuse after his birth had served to reinforce his lack of self-esteem. He said,

The other thing that really, really helped a lot in my healing was learning that I'm something spiritual that is distinct from the physical body. And that was—whew! I can't recall in my life anything that was more profoundly healing than doing that birth regression.

Bruce had taken on the second nature of his mother's guilt and shame. He had also absorbed into his very cells the terror they both felt toward his father. He and his mother were joined together in that way—bound by the guilt and fear of her perceived "sin" and shame.

Just as Sharon understood for the first time that she had taken on her mother's fears, and Ellen slipped out from underneath her mother's depression, Bruce discovered he was a separate, unique person. Each one began to reclaim their "authentic self."

Summing Up

Even before birth, the developing infant's brain is affected by chronic emotional states of the mother. As Gerald Huther and Michael Kohn (2006) write in *The Compassionate Brain*,

> The impact of the environment is dramatic and specific, not merely influencing the general direction of development, but actually affecting how the intricate circuitry of the brain is wired (p. 46).

In the womb, the fetus is learning—not in an intellectual left-brain process, but in a sensory-motor right-brain process—how to deal with life. What he learns lays the groundwork for how he will respond to stressful situations for the rest of his life. To use Lipton's analogy, the melody is laid down in the womb; later, the lyrics must fit that melody (2014). How important it is, then, that pregnant women realize that their babies are listening and learning. If they did, they could find innumerable ways of insuring their messages become endless melodies that bless and comfort their children.

Research indicates that when there is prenatal anxiety and fear, the brain develops in certain ways in order to compensate and handle stress-related hormones of the mother (Antonelli, 2015). Data also reveals that after the fetus experiences prenatal stress (and fear is certainly stressful), the fetus's brain may be less able to effectively handle stress and may be more sensitive to pain and emotional angst after birth. Early formative experiences set up a reactive pattern in the infant's body and mind. Gradually, anxiety can be expected as a part of daily life, just as breathing out and breathing in become normal. In the words of Dr. Ludwig Janus (1997) of Heidelberg, Germany,

> The conditions that prevail at the beginning of life thus acquire a particular importance in that this is what essentially shapes our feeling of self-esteem and the way we experience life, and forms the basis of our later attitude toward ourselves and towards life (p. 62).

To best ensure survival, nature has hardwired the human fetus to react to his environment. The fetus is literally in tune with his mother's physical, emotional, intellectual, and spiritual realities. He begins to learn what he will be "fixing to face" through his mother. If she is frightened, he learns to be afraid. If she is angry, he learns to be angry or to defend himself against her. If she is peaceful and happy, he learns the world he faces will be a welcoming, safe one. Beliefs learned in the womb become a reflexive way of responding to life, a second nature to the infant.

While in a deep, altered state of consciousness, many of my clients tune in to those melodies laid down in the womb and discover they have lived out the lyrics. When they free themselves from old feelings, attitudes, and even basic life patterns they have taken on from parents, particularly the mother, they often feel as if they are being born again or as if they are giving themselves a new beginning.

Mahler, Pine, and Bergman (1975) have described the two types of births, physical and psychological, in this way:

> A number of struggles in life could be categorized as the attempt to be truly "born," to become truly awake. The biological birth of the human infant and the psychological birth of the individual are not coincidental time. The former is a dramatic, observable, and well circumscribed event, the latter a slowly unfolding intra-psychic process (p.12).

The words of e. e. cummings (1938) speak to the importance of psychological birth: "We can never be born enough. We are human beings; for whom birth is a supremely welcome mystery, the mystery of growing: the mystery which happens only and whenever we are faithful to ourselves" (p.4)

3

Breathless:

The Dire Consequences of PSS

I took a deep breath and listened to the old brag off my heart.
I am, I am, I am.

SYLVIA PLATH, *The Bell Jar*

A generation ago, much of the advanced technological knowledge and support that we now take for granted was unavailable during pregnancies and births. There were no sonograms to determine the health and sex of the infant and no sophisticated monitors to register fetal distress, including fetal distress caused by oxygen deprivation. Many newborns who experienced oxygen deprivation during that era are now adults who suffer from Prenatal Suffocation Syndrome (PSS).

Under normal circumstances, during gestation, fetuses live on a quarter of their mother's oxygen supply, which Arthur Janov PhD has said is the equivalent of living on the top of Mount Everest without oxygen cylinders (Janov, 2011). Biologically, the fetus must learn to adapt to the environment of the mother. However, there are many ways a fetus's oxygen supply can be further diminished during gestation and labor without the outside world being aware of the stress on the occupant of the womb. Some causes that compromise oxygen supply to the baby are maternal smoking, alcohol intake, drug addiction, anemia, and blood capacity. Oxygen supply can also be compromised if the umbilical cord is wrapped around the baby's neck, if the cord is kinked, or if the baby is born prematurely. Also, many drugs used to relieve pain during labor have been found to increase the risk of neonatal apnea.

Research has also determined that fear or panic in the mother affects the blood supply to the womb. In addition, some studies have shown that the infant is affected positively or negatively by the chemistry of the mother's emotional state, especially when there is chronic stress. Intense fear or anger in the mother can set up a flight or fight syndrome, which may cause a lessoning of blood supply to the uterus, resulting in oxygen deprivation to the fetus. Anyone who has ever experienced the fear of suffocation, or had to hold his breath under water for too long, has felt how frightening a lack of oxygen can be. The fear escalates, as the length of time without breath increases.

Over one hundred years ago, Sigmund Freud described what we now diagnose as PTSD:

> The memory of trauma…acts like a foreign body which long after its entry must be regarded as an agent that is still at work. It may be said that ideas which have become pathological have persisted with freshness and affective strength because they have been denied the normal wearing away processes by means of abreaction and reproduction in states of uninhibited associations (Freud & Breuer, 1895/2000, p.28).

Only in recent history have we validated that wars leave thousands of veterans not only with physical wounds but also with real mental and emotional wounds. What is less recognized is the traumatization of infants and children, especially in the womb. Like veterans of wars, infants and children who have experienced fear of PSS have PTSD symptoms that can be triggered and cause a response as if it were the original circumstance. A sudden loud noise may cause a veteran with

PTSD to feel and behave as if he were back in a war zone. If a child who had an early trauma of being trapped in the birth canal is held down or smothered while playing, the response may be a thrashing, screaming panic attack related to the original trauma, which clearly was not a game.

I first heard about Prenatal Suffocation Syndrome at a psychology conference seminar given by Dr. William Hull. Prenatal Suffocation Syndrome is a term for the experience of apnea, a temporary cessation of breathing, which can be very frightening. If the experience has been prolonger and traumatizing, it creates a syndrome—an automatic set of responses that can be terrifying. It may create a reaction in the brain that continuously feels as though one is in danger. The brain acts as if there is always the likelihood of a threat. Of course, if breathing stops completely, the result is death.

People who suffer from extreme trauma involving PSS find it very difficult to relax. They are almost always on guard and fear being trapped.

Dr. Hull had been working for decades at an alcoholic treatment center. I was shocked when he said, "I have never met an alcoholic who did not have PSS." Hull explained that

> shortage of oxygen causing stress to the fetus may occur at any time during gestation, including during a trauma the mother is experiencing…When the lack of oxygen is severe, there is trauma for the baby. The fear of not being able to breathe again can be triggered by a host of ordinary occurrences—driving through a tunnel, being caught in a crowd, even wearing a turtleneck sweater. Anything could ignite that sense of being trapped, coupled with a compulsive need to escape (Hull, 1986, p.112).

At any age, all human beings in danger seek some way to protect themselves. Defenses usually involve some form of fight, flight, or freeze, and like Freud's "foreign body," they persist. We create defenses to cope with and repress the accompanying emotional pain. The original terrifying event may have been dismissed as being of no consequence. But nothing can be further from the truth, especially if the trauma occurred in the immature developing brain and went beyond the infant's level of tolerance. The body remembers, and the brain adjusts.

Many of my clients who have experienced a major loss of oxygen in the womb or during birth live their adult life with "one foot out the door." They are watching, expecting, and preparing for some threat to their survival. Living trapped in a nervous response to life, they are always on guard. The body/mind has not recorded the story of why, but the unconscious and body remember in order to guard against "it" happening again.

Some babies who became enraged and fought their way out of the birth canal discover the power of angry energy. Blustering and pushing others out of their way, they subsequently elbow their way through life. Anger becomes their ally as they hide from the deep terror within. They may even overreact when another driver cuts them off on the road.

Other infants during birth struggled and collapsed, then struggled and collapsed again, until finally they gave up. They did not know if or how they would be rescued, but they were born and given the necessary help for survival. However, the imprint of the trauma also survives, and survival patterns cast a long shadow into the future.

In time, we are likely to be defending our defenses, and this may continue for years, even when there isn't any current danger and we, as adults, could be making healthier choices. We project our ancient fears on something or someone in present time. That someone can be our own self, and we can attack with an internalized voice of blame, shame, and worthlessness. Or we might develop numerous stress-related somatic problems. Coping methods may include numbing out, disassociation, sudden uncontrollable rages, addictions, or a rigid attempt to be perfect and in control. Our bodies, as well as our relationships, bear the burden.

Birth is one of the most significant events in life and often can be life threatening to the infant as well as to the mother. Habits such as mindlessly charging ahead, procrastinating, self-sabotage, fears of intimacy, and a host of anxieties and compulsions may have their roots in the infant's struggle to be born. Feelings of claustrophobia can stem from an unconscious body memory of the very real experience of being stuck in the birth canal with the cord wrapped around one's neck.

Scott

The imprint of Scott's birth trauma created a pattern of great beginnings followed by hasty retreats, as if there were some invisible force about to trap him. The pattern lasted many years and, in time, its repetition caused depression and a general defeatist attitude with a serious lack of self-confidence. This was Scott's state of mind when he came to a seventeen-day STAR intensive workshop.

Scott was in his late forties, a tall, handsome, and very gifted African American man who was depressed and discouraged about starting yet another project. After a very promising beginning, he had given up his dreams of being a musician. He recalled what had happened when he had been invited to play at Carnegie Hall when he was a teen. "I choked, it was difficult, and I barely managed to finish."

Charming and intelligent, Scott went into sales. He would quickly become the top salesperson wherever he worked. Just as quickly, he became restless and dissatisfied and quit in a fog of rationalized excuses and self-reproach. He repeated this pattern over and over again.

> I would get to a certain place and get very excited and motivated, and I would move ahead. Then something would happen: I would feel paralyzed in terms of being able to do anything, and I would get depressed. Then, I would just stop.

The story behind his birth might have had an influence on the start-stop pattern he experienced throughout his life, but this notion had never been considered. Birth traumas rarely are. How could Scott's birth experience have affected his work habits almost fifty years later? Impossible, some might protest. Actually, it had everything to do with the way he lived his life.

Scott ran away from situations that might have trapped him, regardless of whether there was any real danger. The imprinting of the original threat at birth coupled with his imagination made the threat *feel* real. The pattern had been established: he felt it and believed it. Driven by what was repressed in his unconscious, he learned to escape in advance.

In a therapy session, Scott re-experienced the absolute panic he felt being born. His body expressed it: he thought he was suffocating. He instinctively felt that to survive, he had to move forward and get out, but when he tried, he was overwhelmed by the sensation of suffocation. Curled up and gasping for breath, he felt the trauma of his birth. He had been unable to escape, and his survival was threatened. He was expressing the many emotions of his unresolved trauma.

The support staff and I sat quietly, not wanting to disturb him. We were mindful that there is often a quiet, reflective time following such deep emotional release, a reflective time that often reveals profound insights and connections. Ideally there are two staff members providing support during a birth regression, and sometimes a third, who might be in training. All of us are skilled at supporting, being observant, and not interfering.

Gradually, he began to relax and then said, "My mother used to talk about that [his birth] a lot. I was born with the umbilical cord around my throat. Born blue or dead, actually. They took me away from her for forty-eight hours."

Some relief and bonding could have been provided if he had been placed in the arms of his mother to be calmed and soothed by her familiar voice, the presence of her smell, her touch, and her love. Instead, he was separated from his mother and felt alone, abandoned, and afraid. Denied everything biology had programmed him to receive, he was learning what to expect from life.

Scott's birth trauma left him with the fear of being hopelessly trapped and with a compulsive, unconscious need to escape. The cord had been wrapped around his neck, and when he pushed forward, it may have tightened, further limiting his oxygen and imprinting him with a compelling fear of going forward. Yet if he did not move forward, he might not escape the narrow confines of the birth canal, and he might die. He experienced an impossible paradox: if you stay here, you may die; if you move forward, you may die. He nearly did. Scott was fighting for his life.

From this experience in the womb, Scott learned to be fearful of changes. Change could be followed by panic, the possibility of further struggle, or the failure to survive at all. Then, over time, Scott's unconscious fears left patterns that were real and active in his life, influencing his choices, behaviors, and emotional state on a day-to-day basis. Caves, closed-in places, even controlling bosses and smothering relationships—all had the power to trigger his birth trauma and his need to escape.

Healing through Therapy and Insight

Without understanding the real reason for the fears, Scott made up "reasonable" excuses, as we all do, and which we then believe. But by understanding the root cause of his fears and his patterns of starting and stopping, Scott gained insight into his behaviors and, perhaps more significantly, a positive feeling about himself. Once he understood that his birth experience was the template for his patterns of behavior, he could address other issues, such as the rage he tightly held inside. After further therapeutic work enabled him to understand, express, and release that rage, he could leave it behind. His new life took off.

Scott best described the change. "I used to say, 'What is wrong with me?' That was always the voice in me. Now I say, 'I'm not defective.' 'I'm not crazy.' 'I am not mentally ill.' 'I am not screwed up.' 'I just had this experience that was real.'"

Scott was elated to learn the logical origin of his irrational behavior. His new understanding empowered him to move ahead in his life and experience the rewards of completion and success.

Now I see the whole birth experience as an incredible teacher for me. I can imagine people who are in prisons, or people [who are] deeply depressed and have given up on themselves because there is something in them that says, 'You can't do it. 'Stop before you die.' They don't know their birth trauma is still with them. I can imagine if they just knew what I know, if they got a bit freed up from it, they would change forever.

I've been able to look at racism in a different way, too, in that I just assumed I was always going to have a hard time as a black man. I felt there was nothing I could do about that either. Even though racism does exist, and sometimes I do catch hell, it doesn't stop me like it used to.

I feel very much freed up from it [old behaviors] now. That feeling of stuckness still comes up, but I feel that I can pull it off, and I can say, 'Oh, that's what it was' and move forward through it. I've committed myself to really finishing learning how to play the guitar in the way I want to play. I feel like I can do that.

Scott is finely free to live his life. He works successfully both as an entertainer and as a facilitator of programs to further interracial understanding and nonviolent conflict resolution.

Emily

Like Scott, Emily frequently found herself unable to move forward in her life. A sense of powerlessness over her circumstances would keep her from reaching personal goals, so she sought therapy to remedy this.

As we worked together, Emily's lifelong fear of suffocation and recurring panic attacks surfaced. Throughout her childhood, Emily would awaken in the middle of the night gasping for air. She would throw open a window, sucking in the fresh air, until her panic subsided. At other times, stressful events literally "took her breath away." I helped Emily return to the time when she first felt this suffocation. She traced the feeling back to the womb, which she described as "like being inside a wet balloon."

Emily later asked her mother about her birth. Her mother explained that two weeks before she was born, the amniotic sac had broken and the fluid had drained away. The doctor decided not to intervene, but rather to wait until the labor began on its own. For two long weeks, Emily was trapped, terrified, and struggling to breathe. She was also unable to move, as she was no longer buoyed in the natural fluid of the womb.

In due time, Emily was born a healthy seven-and-a-half-pound baby. No one could see that she was traumatized and damaged, because her wounds were not physical; instead, they were psychological scar-like impressions of her trauma in the womb. Her fears cast a shadow of anxiety and affected her relationships. In particular, the fear of being trapped again continued to haunt her. The experience had further taught her that when circumstances became difficult, even intolerable, she didn't have any power to change them, so she would simply give up and stop. Then, she would just wait and wait, until eventually something would happen.

The opportunity to relive her birth experience was a turning point for Emily. Now able to recognize the origins of her symptoms, Emily could lay them to rest. She no longer wakes in the night, gasping for air, and she is now able to take risks and be more proactive in her life.

Emily continued to work with me on and off for several years. One of the last times we met, I witnessed an extraordinary spiritual event. I sat beside Emily on the mat, and she easily regressed into a deep meditative state. I could sense she was drifting far away. She neither spoke nor moved for a long time. Then, with almost minute precision, she slowly began to gently twist her body. She squirmed slightly into a curl, as if she wanted to be smaller. Finally, with a huge sigh, she relaxed her body and rested. After a few moments, she began tapping her hands on her chest and said, "Now, this is me. This is Emily." She went on to whisper, "And whatever that was, it was almost on the edge of my consciousness."

After a while, she sat up and told me this account of what had happened. She had been in a space of pure energy and pure peace, at one with the universe in a soft, radiant light. Then she knew she had to squeeze into a body, which was much smaller than she was, and finally she came through. I asked her if she had ever felt that feeling of pure bliss before.

> Yes. When I was a child, I would go out in my backyard to the lawn. I would stretch out my arms and begin to twirl. I would twirl and twirl as fast as I could until I fell back on the grass. Then I would feel it again. I could actually hear the breeze pass over me. I would feel the peace and know who I was.

Anita

The symptoms of unrecognized birth trauma can take many forms, but for Anita, there weren't any obvious symptoms. Like Emily's trauma, Anita's trauma went unacknowledged until she entered therapy with me.

A slight, pretty woman in her late thirties, Anita attended a lecture I gave in Europe on pre- and perinatal psychology, and she was drawn to what she heard that evening. She felt a need to pursue her own earliest experiences and made an appointment to see me.

In our session, Anita easily and deeply regressed to her birth. This was a profound experience for both of us. Without saying a word, her body began to express the terrifying sensations of PSS that she had experienced when she was being born. I watched as Anita went through the stages of struggling, giving up, gasping, and intermittently erupting in rage. A number of times her body writhed, and finally, with a lurch, seemed to be out of the torture of the birth canal.

Because I would soon be leaving for California, we arranged to work together again the following day. Our second meeting was very similar to the first, and it was just as powerful. Her terror was palpable.

After the session, she sat quietly, absorbing what had happened. Then she looked at me and said, "That's why I've been afraid to have children. I never wanted anyone to have to go through that." She had had several abortions in the past and had justified each one for ecological and political reasons—any reason other than the one she discovered through regression. The unconscious memory of her own birth was in her body and her psyche, and because of it, she feared giving birth to such an extent that, at thirty, she elected to have a hysterectomy to avoid ever becoming pregnant again. As she softly cried, she told me about her lifelong fear of relationships.

Although the damage caused by Anita's birth trauma was not obvious, it devastated her life and crippled her potential. It had created an unconscious pattern that prohibited meaningful relationships or a sense of belonging. She had never been able to stay with anybody or anything for any length of time—a common pattern in adults who have experienced PSS. Anita lived a nomadic life, frequently changing location, work, and relationships to avoid the possibility of being "trapped" as she had been in the birth canal. She told me, "I will begin a new job or a new relationship, and soon I will begin to feel claustrophobic, so I leave. Over and over again, I haven't ever stayed in one place very long."

Doing corrective birth imagery work with Anita, I guided her through imagining a positive birth. She envisioned and felt positive pictures of wriggling her way out, breathing easily, and enjoying the warm, loving arms of her mother. In doing this, she created a new way of dealing with the previously unconscious memory of her birth trauma.

Following the imagery work, I asked her what her life might have been like if she had been born as she had just imagined. "Oh, if I had been born like that, I would have felt like I had a place on the planet. I would belong! I would have been able to do so much good for so many people. I wouldn't have been so serious and heavy. I would have let myself have a good life, have joy, not all this suffering."

Summing Up

There aren't any statistics showing how much damage very early psychological wounds do to an individual's self-esteem and quality of life. We have statistics concerning the physical damage of birth traumas, but emotional and mental damage usually go unrecognized.

However, when we look at the lives of Scott, Emily, and Anita, we have an inkling of what can be lost for them, for their families and friends, and for all of us because of early wounding. Research says we use only a fraction of our human potential. It is likely that early traumas, abuse, and deprivation contribute to what is lost. Many who are badly traumatized in the womb or during birth never bloom. They never feel like they belong, are worthy, or able to "do much good." There is a stranglehold on their freedom to become all they were created to be.

Scott, Emily, and Anita represent many others whose ever-present but invisible wounds jeopardize their well-being and self-esteem. In the end, we all pay the price of our blindness, our lack of understanding, and our denial of the pivotal role our first experiences play in the shaping of our destiny.

The most important time to significantly influence the path of a human life is at its beginning. Mistakes made then can drastically change the direction and the quality of life, individually and collectively. Uncorrected, one mistake brings on others, the crisis escalates, and the psyche cascades into chaos. As was true for Donna (whose story is told in chapter 2), not a single aspect of Anita's life—intellectual, physical, emotional, social, or spiritual—escaped the shock and terror of her birth.

Life for each of the individuals in this chapter would have been much different had the invisible psychological wounds of their birth traumas been recognized and acknowledged. All birth trauma wounds can potentially be put in check.

Fortunately, regression therapy enables those who struggle with the aftermath of birth trauma to return to those experiences to understand them and the impact they have on their lives. The debilitating effects can be overcome, as the experiences of Scott, Emily, and Anita show. Even in far more damaging cases such as Donna's, there is still an opportunity to correct the results of those early errors.

It is not too late for anyone to reclaim his or her life, learn to relax, and live with a sense of inner peace. Nor is it too late for all of us to seriously examine attitudes and practices around birth. Whenever there has been oxygen deprivation, we need to take the necessary steps to prevent additional suffering or unfortunate consequences.

Clearly, the most effective way to blunt or erase the long-lasting traces of birth trauma is at the beginning. The newborn and the mother should be given time to be together to bond and create a secure attachment that erases trauma. Supporting such a simple, profoundly powerful time of connection and love is so easy and not expensive. When we do that, we affirm nature's blessing, which in turn sustains the life and spirit of infant and mother.

4

The Power of Attachments: Someone or Something to Hold Onto

Children have a biological instinct to attach. They have no choice. Whether their parents or caregivers are loving and caring, or distant, insensitive, rejecting or abusive, children will develop a coping style based on their attempt to get at least some of their needs met…they will find other ways. Anything is preferable to that God forsaken sense of irrelevance and alienation.

BESSEL VAN DER KOLK

Many people who have experienced entrapment and oxygen deprivation at birth later exhibit an overwhelming need to escape from what they perceive to be confining situations. "I must get out of here" is their cry. Their early survival imprints become habituated ways of thinking and behaving, which endure long after the original episode. Confronted with later events approximating the original scenario, the old script replays and duplicates the actions and emotions from the original trauma experienced at birth. This is the essence of posttraumatic stress disorder (PTSD.) Previous traumas provide the template that later feelings and actions fit into.

Fight, flee, or freeze are the biological defenses that were useful to our ancestors to escape from lions, and they remain useful to us now when there is a real threat. But damage occurs when we live as if the lion is about to pounce at any moment. This stance brings stress, strains our relationships, compromises our immune systems, and damages our health, both physically and emotionally. Much harm comes from living on the edge as we fearfully wait, expecting only the worst, trusting only our defenses, and projecting our fears and expectations on someone or something until we are taking action as if it were true. We sabotage opportunities, relationships, and well-being, and we rarely relax unless we drink or use drugs, recreational or otherwise. We may also shut down or zone out with TV and the Internet. Making commitments and staying on the job or in one place or with one person too long is apt to feel risky and can trigger the escape button. We are compelled by the past to repeat our history, since we respond to our perception of reality rather than to what is actually happening in the present. Believing becomes more real than seeing.

Whenever old trauma is restimulated, the individual's body "remembers" and responds with the same physical and emotional reactions as in the initial trauma. The belief that "it" might be happening again is so deeply held in the unconscious that the illusion seems real. A person suffering from claustrophobia may try to persuade himself that going through a tunnel is safe, but the power of the unconscious supersedes the present-day intellect. Such is the force of hidden fear born out of trauma. The conscious mind may have forgotten, but the unconscious does not forget. It waits on guard and is poised to urge escape if anything close to entrapment and suffocation seems eminent. The body remembers.

As an individual leaves childhood and enters adulthood, the instinctive survival patterns become more sophisticated but continue to maintain an unconscious grip. Whatever the method of escape used, justifications and reasons for escaping can be found, even if the reasons are not rational or logical. Patterns imprinted so early with ancient fears don't leave any options for reasoning. Any excuse works in moments of panic. The overwhelming motivation is simply to escape. The bottom line is to avoid ever getting stuck again, suffocating, and possibly dying. Hypervigilance often becomes the norm and feels as comfortable as old slippers. In this hypervigilant state, even when relaxation comes, there is usually some degree of anxiety. Peace actually feels dangerous, like not being in control. Instead, being on guard feels safe. The fear of entrapment and suffocation becomes free-floating and unanchored from any awareness of the original cause. Eventually, it becomes fear of being afraid, with a prerequisite to be vigilant and in control.

However, some people who suffer from early trauma never recognize or show any signs of fear. Living on the edge and liking it, they carry a façade of bravado. They are most threatened when faced by intimacy. Feelings of the heart and the language of love are dangerous territory. Sex may be easy, but loving is not. Quite often, their experience as infants included a lack of bonding with parents or caregivers.

The human desire to attach to a safe person is a built-in, mammalian survival need. Ideally, the connection is made with another human being, preferably the mother. When that connection can't be found or trusted, an individual may seek any substitute to fill the void and instead may bond with a negative self-concept, an addiction, a false persona, an irrational allegiance to a cause, even a physical problem or pain. Some connection is essential. Anything is better than that unbearable feeling of being immaterial or worthless.

In the absence of consistent, safe, and loving human beings, young children often bond to a pet, a place, an imaginary friend who is always available, or an object, such as a stuffed teddy bear, a special doll, or a blanket, which then becomes their most treasured belonging. They cling to it for security and comfort, just as the Peanuts character Linus does with his blanket. Many parents have had to confront an angry, fearful, or heartbroken child when the child's special "blankie" was lost, laundered, or, God forbid, thrown away. Without the beloved object, the child may feel afraid, lost, or more alone.

I once had a client who as a child found his secure connection with a beautiful tree in his back yard. He felt safe and welcome in the branches of that tree. One day he came home from school to find it had been cut down. He sat on a stump and sobbed his heart out. His father laughed at him and said, "It is only a tree." No! It was not only a tree to the little boy. It was his safe connection. It was his secure attachment object.

On another occasion, I knew a family who left the child's favorite teddy bear in a motel. Upon realizing they had left it, they turned the car around and drove back fifty miles to get it. Luckily, it was still there. Other, less compassionate parents might have said, "You have other ones," and driven on, oblivious to the child's feelings of panic and devastation.

Unfortunately, insensitivity or lack of awareness can seem rampant. One client I knew adored a pet dog that had serious health issues. An acquaintance asked her, "Why are you spending all this time and money on a dog? Just go get another one." The suggestion of "go get another one," be it a beloved dog or a treasured teddy bear, means the person making the suggestion doesn't understand. It is not the same! The individual's sense of security and well-being is at stake.

David

David came to STAR to work on life-long patterns of self-sabotage and to recover from a traumatic robbery experience. As a child, he had been the identified "patient" of his family. He told me, "My sister was and is a very beautiful, simplistic, easy-going person. All the family anger and punishment went to me. She was never punished. I was the 'little son of a bitch,' and I got it. I was yelled at to go to my room. 'Get in there!' All I wanted was to be accepted."

As a way of escaping his painful family dynamic, he would withdraw to his room and listen to baseball games on his beloved Zenith radio.

That hard-box transistor radio, rather than a soft, cuddly teddy bear, was David's chosen security object. It brought him comfort and safety, and it became his ticket to escape to a happier place, which was what mattered most to him.

Years passed, and when it was time for David to go to college, of course the transistor radio would be going along. However, when he arrived at the dorm, the radio was no longer with him. Frantic phone calls home followed, but no one could find the radio. The high degree of David's upset was genuine. In his words, "I was distraught when I lost it." He had lost his treasured "radio friend" who had nurtured him throughout his childhood. Gone was his means of escaping pain and loneliness. He no longer had something that was singularly "his."

Later, as an adult, David transferred those feelings to his car, which became his new "feel good, escape ticket." The dynamics were the same. When he found himself in difficult situations and lacked alternative coping skills, his old panic surfaced. Now he ran, not to the comfort of his Zenith radio, but to his car. For David, the Zenith radio escape became the fast car escape. The characters, set, and dialogue shifted, but the plot remained the same. He had grown up with his rage, distrust, and need to escape intact. A self-identified "great escape artist," he was ever ready to rescue himself from any perceived threats, especially those that seemed to emanate from other people. As he reported, "I have a distrust and cynicism for people. I always feel people have a motive, an ulterior reason, and by God, I'm going to figure out what that damned reason is. I've put cynicism into my survival bag." His trust rested in his old survival methods. Certainly, "trust in others" was not in his bag.

As a young man, David went to Hollywood to follow his dream of being a film editor. There he married, had children, worked with famous directors, and began to make a name for himself. However, old unconscious patterns plagued him in the form of multiple affairs with women and angry outbursts. As David explained, "If I felt any movement was restricted, the only way I knew I'd get out was through violence. Anger often supplied the energy to accomplish that goal."

His anger and inability to control his rage led to his being fired. Unable to find work, he panicked and fled to Detroit, where his father lived. His father gave him a job sorting dirty linen in his commercial cleaning business. It was difficult, sweaty, miserable work, and a far stretch from his Hollywood days. David put up with it as long as he could before asking his father to move him into the pressing room. He was told, "You'll stay where I tell you to until I'm good and ready!" What a putdown and what a challenge! Once again, he found himself stuck in a miserable place. Feeling he didn't have any choice or any power, his early trauma was activated. When his father confronted him with orders to stay where he was, David's anger flared with a "Fuck you! I'm out of here!" His anger only intensified, and he escaped.

In a matter of a few weeks, David had gone from film editing in Hollywood to sorting dirty sheets in a hellhole. There was little space for logic. Neither his rational intelligence nor his higher consciousness had any room to intervene. As David said, "I get overwhelmed, and I can't tell fantasy from reality. I rise to anger. There is no reasoning with me."

Six weeks later, he was back in Hollywood. He said, "I continued with my explosive rage, burning every bridge until there were no more opportunities. I turned down an offer to work on the movie Rocky to work instead for my mother in her business, which I hated. My mind was made up, so I said no to Rocky." As is common among people who are trapped in old patterns, there wasn't any flexibility in his mind-set. He couldn't reason with himself or with others. Instead, he would vehemently defend irrational decisions, no matter how destructive they were. In such cases, it is as if the individual's preference is to be right about the chosen set of defenses rather than risk choosing a different response. David was simply reacting with and reliving an old pattern of survival.

Later, he sat in Florida and watched an old friend accept an Academy Award for editing Rocky. He was angry and hated himself. He fought with his mother, divorced his wife, separated from his children, and acted out sexually. He was totally miserable.

He stayed in Florida for twenty years, dependent on his mother for a job he hated, until a robbery shook him to his roots. Three armed men broke into his mother's store and beat him up. Then they tied him up and locked him in a small bathroom in the back of the store. As David lay there hopelessly struggling to get free, terror seized him. He was helpless, terrified, and unable to move. The power of his anger could not free him. Exhausted and traumatized, he finally collapsed on the cold floor and fell asleep. He said, "During the robbery which was probably, ultimately, a real-life, true reenactment of what happened at birth, I was overwhelmed. I tried to get out and couldn't. I rocked, and I rocked, and I rocked until I was exhausted. I ended up falling asleep." When he awoke, he still faced his deepest fear—total helplessness and vulnerability—similar feelings to those he had felt during his birth.

He had spent most of his life avoiding feeling vulnerable by escaping, or masking it with rage, which gave him an illusion of power. However, always underneath this illusion of power was his terror of never escaping and dying, completely helpless.

There on the bathroom floor, he was alert in case he needed to fight, flee, or freeze. None of these options were available to him. All were methods of escape from what he unconsciously feared might happen again—to be trapped as he had been during his birth. It was happening again! His greatest, though unconscious, issue was surfacing again! He believed the robbers would kill him.

David's Birth Trauma

In many ways, the trauma David experienced during the robbery restimulated his birth trauma. Life's first threat had come to David during his birth, when a feeling of being trapped and of being without oxygen terrified him. He felt he was suffocating and in danger of dying.

During his birth regression, David again experienced breathlessness and an intense terror of suffocation along with severe pain. He physically felt as if he could no longer breathe. The old trauma was restimulated, and his body "remembered" and responded with the same physical and emotional reactions as in the initial trauma. He said later, "It seems like there were times I could breathe, and then there were times I was suffocating."

The easiest thing to do was to play dead, but David escaped through violence—he withdrew, curled up, gathered strength, and then exploded—which set up a survival pattern and accounted for his frequent hair-trigger explosions. Anger was a powerful defense. It brought him escape from a difficult situation and kept him safe. It also saved him from feeling the deeper, more threatening feeling of vulnerability. Unfortunately, one of the greatest losses in living like this is the crippling of the energies of the heart. One's ability to give and receive love requires being vulnerable, but for victims of prenatal suffocation syndrome (PSS), love becomes dangerous, and fear becomes safe.

Later in his life, as others do when under great threat, he fell back on the survival methods he had learned as far back as in the womb. Whenever pressure became unbearable, David fought back. "I felt I had the power to kick and push, and I did, and I would. I will fight!" As an adult, he ruined his film career and many relationships by this pattern of behavior. He was always too quick to fight. It was an instinctually programmed reaction to "tight corners." He responded, even before he needed to respond, in an old reactive pattern "just in case."

I replicated that pattern so much in my life—it's as if I wanted to do it again. I take everything to the edge. Be it school, or be it personal relationships, I take it to the edge to see if my survival tactics work. It's been that way forever, and it's obviously self-destructive.

It was obviously self-destructive when he told me about it, but once upon a time, a very long time ago, it had saved him from suffocating. He had fought in order to escape danger at birth.

The consequences of this survival imprint for David could be seen in a string of failed relationships, ongoing stress, loss of any kind of intimacy, and missed opportunities, with little awareness of alternative methods of response. For David, as is true for others, imprinted survival behaviors became automatic reactions, activating old response patterns without any pause to reflect and make a better choice. As David said, "The imprint of what happened to me is so deep in my cells—of that violence and that terror—that the feelings overwhelm me. Sometimes I can't distinguish reality from fantasy."

The anticipation of something that might be threatening could trigger his need to escape or to express rage. He lived on the alert in order to avoid re-experiencing the possibility of entrapment and suffocation that he had felt during birth and that continued to exist in his unconscious mind as an ever-present possibility. When his mind was on red alert, the line between what was real or present and what was not could be instantly swept away by a flood of fear. Furthermore, when deeply confronted with fear, David had developed excellent rationalizations to explain his behavior and lack of impulse control.

A More Evolved Path

David's difficulty in life was not being able to see beyond the limited success of his defenses or challenge his belief that they were the only options available for dealing with his problems. He didn't consider any other possibilities, such as negotiating, communicating, or compromising. As a result, a trail of broken relationships, incomplete tasks, and lost opportunities, both personally and professionally, were left in his wake. It was as if he still lived his life controlled by his unconscious fear of being stuck in the birth canal.

A more evolved path is the one David finally chose. By going back into the original trauma, releasing his repressed feelings, then understanding his patterns, he now has the conscious awareness and the courage to choose new, healthier, and more positive responses to his old, reactive, habituated model. After all, at fifty-six, he is no longer in the birth canal. And he knows it! Having gained awareness, he is now able to see things from a different perspective. He has a more genuine self-esteem, if not a gentle appreciation of the defenses that were originally a service to him.

As tragic and frightening as it was, the robbery threw him into the terror he had avoided all his life. In that extreme re-enactment of his original pain, indeed, in the darkness of the robbery's terror, he unwittingly began to find his way to freedom. At fifty, on the floor of the bathroom where the robbers had confined him, he had been struggling, unable to break free.

In therapy, when David experienced the terror, rage, and helplessness of his own birth, he saw the influence his unconscious survival patterns had on his life. By becoming conscious of what had been running his life, he discovered he could learn a new and healthier repertoire of responses.

A therapist had once asked him, "Why don't you do what you really want to do in life?" David had answered, "Those things are not in my realm." He has since moved to another state and found a community of friends and fulfilling work. Many things that were not in his "realm" before currently are an integral part of his life.

David also had an opportunity during therapy to strengthen his new awareness and resolve. He developed a parallel memory to counter the old script that had previously taunted him. By crawling through a mock birth tunnel, he had a somatic and a psychological opportunity to correct the old pattern and reinforce his new approach to life. It was a healing and affirming experience for him. He said,

> Redoing the pattern in the birth tunnel gave me a chance to start believing in a parallel memory. It was wonderful. I could start to see that I could use the pressure around my legs and not fight it, to let it be there, and feel it. I actually started to feel good on my third time through. I could use it to my advantage. I've not used things to my advantage. Obviously, as a result of my birth, I overreact.

By actually squirming through the tunnel, his body and mind began to record the possibility of living in a different way.

Now that I'm able to say, "I truly like me," it feels like one of those big old skeleton keys opening that big door, and saying, "God, this guy is okay." The desire to be free and stand in my own power has obviously been there from birth. I fight and give it up. Maybe now I can just accept and be at peace with myself.

Summing Up

Many clients feel that a way of being or feeling has been with them "forever." The word "forever" is a clue to how early the pattern began, deeper than any conscious memory, and earlier than any verbal or cognitive development.

Like subliminal messages, survival messages learned early in life are embedded in our unconscious mind and rule our behavior, attitudes, and actions. The original trauma that taught us about survival may not be consciously seen or understood. We rationalize, justify, and explain our behavior in countless ways, and our feelings then support our perceptions and behavior. Meanwhile, the lessons we learned in the womb and during birth and infancy replay over and over in mild or intense ways, even for years. They become well-worn habits and are referred to as, "Oh, that's just the way I am." There is no desire to change or belief that change is possible. Eventually, exhaustion, illness, rage, or age saps the energy needed to live out the old drama. We may become depressed, withdraw, or dart from one failed attempt to the next, until we give up any hope that our life can be different.

David's story shows how pre- and perinatal traumas can dominate life, relationships, attitudes, and behavior. These traumas form a template that guides later development and casts a long shadow. For that reason, therapists and clients who exclude from therapy experiences from the earliest period of life are only repairing the structure without investigating the foundation. A skilled craftsman may remodel and beautify rooms on the first floor, but if it rests on a rotten foundation, the whole structure is at risk.

David had years of therapy in a desperate attempt to change his behavior and feel better. None of it really helped him. He had learned a few problem-solving skills and appeared better, but inside, all was in continued chaos because his psychological foundation was built on fear. He lived by the framework of a rigidly controlled mind-set, laced with denial, rationalization, and separation.

The power of his perinatal imprints directed his life. It was apparent in his dependence upon using his anger to "get him out" of situations. It was also apparent in his decision to run back to the assumed "safety net" of his father and then of his mother. In both cases, as in his actual birth, those "wombs" were painful and confining. David used his anger to escape from his father's sweatshop, but it took therapy that resolved his birth trauma for him to be able to escape his mother's control.

David had acted out sexually during most of his life, including during his marriages. His unfulfilled biological needs for touch, holding, and affection from his mother were never adequately met. As an adult, he still yearned for what he had missed, and he used sex to meet those needs and receive what he had needed from his mother as a baby. Obviously, this behavior brought only temporary gratification. As David said, "The need still remains unfulfilled. I want to be accepted by my mother. Now, she's eighty-six and I'm fifty-six, and I know she'll never give it to me."

Perhaps he stayed working for her for twenty years in a business he hated because he was still unconsciously hoping to receive what he'd missed as a child. However, what he needed as a baby and did not get from her could not really be satisfied by his experience as an adult.

Are we forever condemned to compulsively seek to fill that bottomless hole in our hearts? The answer is no. There are many ways of dealing with this painful inner emptiness, some of which are healthy and some of which are not. An unhealthy way is to deny and repress all needs. In this case, the individual's relationships are at best comfortable, especially if her partner is also a person who has chosen a similar path of repressing his needs. Another unhealthy way is to never feel fulfilled, but always needy to the point of greed. Even when the individual gets what she thinks she wants, it rarely satisfies the need. If by happenstance, her chosen partner is also very needy, a power struggle ensues. There are no winners in this struggle. At odds with their biology, these individuals live an inauthentic and controlled life, afraid to let go, often even afraid to relax. Intimacy is nearly impossible for them because the requisite vulnerability is so dangerous. They march through their years until they have no energy to maintain the struggle. Their hearts have closed.

Whatever David learned about surviving, he learned long before kindergarten or even before he took his first step or could say his first word. He learned the basic patterns of his later behavior in the birth canal, which he unconsciously, yet faithfully, obeyed for fifty years. The fear and pain of suffocation became his teacher. He said, "It hurt to where I wanted to kill whatever was pushing on my head."

Fight, flight, or freeze—David used each of these reptilian survival-based reactions to dangerous situations. They are built into the part of our brain that is instinctual, and under great stress, we revert to our most primitive defenses. He instinctually chose in the moment what he believed were his best possible defenses. First, because of the pain, he got mad and fought. When that became unsuccessful, he fled. From what, and to where, was almost irrelevant. His last resort was to freeze—to numb out and play dead. When a person spaces out or goes numb, it is a way of freezing, laying low, and hoping the enemy will pass by, just like a turtle or a possum will do.

He continued testing his defenses over and over again to make sure they still worked. He actually felt safer, more alive, and powerful, when he was living on the edge. In this way, he was always prepared. He was always ready to save himself, lest he be caught again in that "hellish, horrendous ordeal."

After birth regression therapy, David told me, "Whew, boy! I know where that terror was conceived. Now it's time to take some of these tools and move on. I feel, 'Ah, there is light.' I see it and I'm going there. If I have that old feeling, I can go ahead, just feel it, and let it go."

5

Cascade into Chaos:
Trauma at Birth

We are all in a post-hypnotic trance induced in early infancy.

R. D. LAING

If miscalculations are made at the launch of a spacecraft, in time the craft will veer farther and farther from its intended path. If the error is great or if there are several errors, the distance between the spacecraft and its destination will become greater. Early detection and correction offer the only hope. Otherwise, the mission will fail.

Pre- and perinatal traumas are comparable to miscalculations made at the beginning of a journey to space. They have the power to alter the course of an individual's development from a life of personal fulfillment to one of travail and misery. As discussed in the previous chapter, an infant's first impressions of life and the *survival messages* imprinted at that time will have a lasting, even permanent impact on the quality of his life. When traumatic, these imprints can cast a shadow on all aspects of the child's future, including the child's relationships, physical and mental health, self-esteem, and attitudes about life.

Recognition and correction of these traumas is essential to helping the individual achieve the best possible therapeutic outcome. As with the navigation of a spacecraft, the earlier corrections are made, the more effective and easier it is to accomplish the original mission.

Our society is showing signs that point to early human miscalculations or missteps. The National Institute of Mental Health's figures that I mentioned in the preface are worth repeating. In 2010, just over 20 percent (or one in five) children either currently have or previously had a seriously debilitating mental disorder (Merikangas et al, 2010). The Center for Disease Control and Prevention reported that in 2013, a total of 13 percent of children ages eight to fifteen had a diagnosable mental disorder the previous year. ADHD and PTSD are now commonly found in children (Centers for Disease Control, n.d.).

In the United States, each year 86,000 women experience an emergency during childbirth (McQueen, 2013). There is a child born every eight seconds in the United States (Dell, n.d.), yet our infant mortality rate of 6.1 deaths per 1000 births is alarming for an industrialized nation (Ingraham, 2014). American women are more likely to die in childbirth than women in any other developed country, which leaves the United States with a rank of 33rd among 179 countries (Robeznicks, 2015). Equally confounding to consider is the global report that a woman dies from pregnancy or childbirth complications every two minutes, and eight hundred women around the world die unnecessarily during pregnancy or childbirth each day (WHO et al, 2014).

Infants in the wombs of those mothers experience those emergencies as well. Babies who are wanted, kept safe in utero, born with minimum pain or trauma, and lovingly welcomed to the world are more likely to grow up to become adults with empathy and compassion. However, those who are unwanted, frightened, or traumatized during the mother's pregnancy begin to defend themselves in the womb. If their birth is traumatic, or if they are separated from their mothers, they are born hypervigilant.

Perhaps their childhood is spent in dangerous circumstances, or they are often hungry and alone. They are statistically more likely to feel hostile, fear others, and become aggressive or withdrawn. Is it any wonder why they join gangs, are violent, or use mind-altering drugs? They are angry and have a good reason to feel that way. They feel cheated, and they were.

Consider again the launch of a spacecraft. Just as the planning and execution of a successful space mission requires an in-depth understanding of the laws of physics, and each stage must be precisely timed, so human gestation, birth, and nurturance must follow Nature's specifications. The infant's well-being depends upon honoring the ancient processes that Nature has designed over eons of time. A spacecraft is a human-made object, designed by brilliant scientists and hardwired for success, but the brilliance of scientists pales when compared to the wisdom of Nature, which has a long, successful history. A human being is a creature designed by Nature and is likewise programmed to succeed. When we, in our arrogance, interfere with Nature, we pay a price.

Similarly, we pay a price if we ignore Nature's wisdom and search for the causes behind disorders such as ADHD, PTSD, drug addiction, suicide, and a host of other problems but do not start our investigation in the womb. Unfortunately, this time of a child's earliest and most powerful learning experiences is usually ignored, though today researchers possess a wealth of information about the emotional and psychological needs of the unborn and newly born baby and the lasting effects of trauma or neglect. When we consider the sharp rise in youngsters with behavior difficulties, including the increasing numbers of children shooting other children, we need to question why and look for trauma experienced in the womb, at birth, and soon after birth.

Over the years, I have met people whose stories of early trauma have tugged at my heartstrings. Beyond that, they have inspired and motivated me to communicate, as widely as possible, the extreme importance of life's early impressions. Time and again I have thought, "If only someone had known what to do, what words needed to be spoken, what simple actions needed to be taken, much harm could have been avoided, and much healing could have been accomplished."

The following story illustrates the consequences of just a few short but critical hours. It is an especially tragic example, not only because of the lasting pain early trauma cast over the woman's life but also because the trauma was completely unnecessary. A series of miscalculations at her birth, one error precipitating the next, cascaded her into a lifetime of chaos and fear.

Donna

I met Donna when she accompanied her twenty-year-old daughter, Patty, to a weeklong workshop I was giving on birth trauma and pre- and perinatal psychology at the Esalen Institute. Donna was tentative, unusually shy, and fearful. She was clearly very concerned and solicitous about her daughter and their relationship. Patty was a tall, slender young woman with beautiful strawberry blond hair. As the week's work unfolded, it became obvious that Patty's difficulties were intricately interwoven with her mother's fears. What occurred fifty long years ago at Donna's birth had surged throughout Donna's life and affected Patty's life; it also touched the lives of Donna's other two daughters.

The workshop was for individuals wishing to explore their own births as well as for professionals interested in learning about pre- and perinatal psychology. It involved both lecture and demonstration sessions, and it showed how regression therapy allows clients and therapists to address early issues and how this affects healing.

Like many who hear about birth traumas and their aftermath, Donna found herself feeling uneasy and anxious as she began to wonder if something from her own past was affecting her present life. She told me, "I have always been frightened, afraid to put myself forward in any way." In addition, throughout her life, she had had chronic and debilitating problems with food and digestion.

Growing up had been a struggle for her, and life continued to be challenging. She was painfully sensitive to her environment and to people. Even mildly stressful situations could overwhelm her. She was curious to learn whether her symptoms—anxiety, lack of self-confidence, environmental sensitivities, and general fragility—might have their origins in her experience of being born.

Several weeks later, Donna made an appointment to see me for therapy in my office. Therapy was not new to Donna. For most of her life, she had been seeing mental health professionals encompassing a variety of approaches including Freudian, Gestalt, Jungian, and other cognitive therapies. In all this work, however, her birth, or its possible impact on her life, had never been mentioned.

One afternoon in therapy, Donna regressed back to her birth. Painful emotions of terror and rage erupted, alternately engulfing her body. In this environment of safety, she released some of this past pain and emotion. After a while, she became quiet and rested. Patients often need a time of stillness after such a catharsis to integrate the experience.

Soon, Donna began to talk to me.

I was born on Christmas in 1945 in a hospital on an army base where my dad was stationed. I know that my parents had to rush to the hospital because all of a sudden my mother started having contractions. It was close to midnight on Christmas Eve when my father brought my mom to the hospital. I was really coming out. My mother literally felt like I was being born just then. The doctor was at a Christmas party, but they located a nurse. Since the doctor wasn't there, the nurse felt obliged to stop the birth process. She immediately put my mother into a bathtub of ice cubes to stop me from being born! I do remember, actually, the feeling of being totally cold and frozen, stuck somewhere. My mother must have been frightened, too, as if something was terribly wrong. They kept us in ice cubes in this bathtub until the doctor showed up.

This was the young army wife's first pregnancy. She and her husband had looked forward excitedly to the arrival of their first baby. Imagine her shock at being thrust into a bathtub filled with ice cubes. Donna's mother was now freezing, confused, alone, and helpless. She didn't know why they were doing this to her. She was not only cold but also terrified—and so was her baby. The contractions abruptly stopped. Was her baby okay? What was wrong? When her labor stopped, she was afraid something terrible had happened to her baby.

Nothing in biology or Nature had prepared either mother or infant for this. What had been proceeding so naturally with great excitement and anticipation became a nightmare. The shock of the cold ice and the insensitive treatment by hospital staff abruptly halted the natural process. Nature was violated. This event was abusive to the laboring mother, her baby, and her husband.

If a gazelle is in labor and senses a lion nearby, her labor will abruptly stop until there is no threat; it is a natural, protective response. But the ice treatment given to Donna's mother was an unnatural interference in the process of Donna's birth. Years later, during a regression to this horrifying experience, shivering from the memory, Donna softly whispered, "Something was terribly wrong." Her assessment was correct. Using the ice cube bath to stop Donna's birth was terribly wrong.

This drastic decision on the part of the medical staff precipitated a series of events. It was not so easy for labor to begin again. By the time the doctor arrived, the young mother was freezing and frightened. Drugs given to the mother to restart contractions also rendered her unconscious. Her baby, Donna, was afraid and did not want to come out. Forceps were used to pull her from the womb. This is, thankfully, less likely to happen in today's medical environment as awareness of the impact on the baby has increased.

The accumulated effects, like dominoes, tumbled Donna into a traumatic abyss of self-doubt, terror, and abandonment from which she rarely escaped. One mistake led to the next, taking her into an endless dark space where there wasn't any safety, comfort, or connection except with her fear. Programmed by Nature to expect to push her way out into the world, she had been thwarted and blocked. Her whole system was overcome with fear, shock, and rage.

> It was easy before, but now I wasn't coming out. So they had to get there with these forceps and get a hold of my head to pull me out. In the process, they hurt me. There are a couple of indentations in my skull that you can still feel.
>
> I was so angry! I mean enraged! A mixture of anger, rage, and terror, all combined. First feeling really cold, really scared, and then being pulled out, which felt like more violence. My birth was stopped. I tried to get this far, and then, "You are wrong!" Halfway down the birth canal, I felt it: "I'm wrong. I made a mistake, and this is the wrong time."

I have seen many regressed clients scream and clasp their heads when they re-experience the agony of being gripped by forceps. One client of mine said, "Birth gives you your first opinion about the planet, what you are up against, and what you are fixing to face."

At this time of vulnerability and brain development, such an experience became an indelible first impression, foreshadowing what Donna was "fixing to face." It was not going to be good. Her life would be a replay of being afraid to move forward, to take risks, and to explore new opportunities. Fear was her constant companion. Being wrong was a core belief. Life was wrong. She was wrong.

Separation after Birth

The events up to this point had been devastating for both mother and infant, physically as well as emotionally. What the parents thought would be a healthy, normal delivery was quite the opposite.

However, the damage to Donna and her mother because of their horrendous experience would have been ameliorated significantly if they had been given the time and opportunity to be together after Donna's birth. Bonding between the nursing mother and child would have occurred through the natural stimuli of the five senses—sight, sound, touch, taste, and smell. Mother and infant would have relaxed, and Donna would have felt safe in her new world. Birth is stressful, and Nature has planned for mother and baby to be together immediately afterward, not only as a pleasant bonding option, but also as an essential step in achieving optimal development. As Jean Liedloff has written in *The Continuum Concept*,

> The feeling appropriate to an infant in arms is his feeling of rightness or essential goodness. The only positive identity he can know, being the animal that he is, is based on the premise that he is right, good, and welcome. Without that conviction, a human being of any age is crippled by a lack of confidence, or a full sense of self, of spontaneity, of grace.[8]

The mother benefits from bonding as well. As Ashley Montagu, an early, eloquent spokesperson for the importance of the mother-infant connection, wrote, "It is clear that the mother needs her baby immediately after birth quite as much as the baby needs her."[9]

Unfortunately, in Donna's case, mistakes continued to be made. Following her birth, Donna was bundled up and taken away to the nursery, and a crucial opportunity for early bonding, as Nature had intended, was irrevocably lost. At that time, Donna desperately needed to be with her mother. Her body and her spirit ached for her mother's eyes, voice, smell, and touch—these are biologically programmed needs, hardwired within a baby's system. But for Donna there was no warm holding and gentle bonding, no soft, soothing sounds of her mother's heart and voice, no touch to welcome her into the world, to lessen her terror and relax her body. The one person in the universe who was biologically programmed to protect her, reassure her, and make her feel safe was not available. Her mother, her world, and her safety net had disappeared.

I don't know if my mother ever saw me. She was drugged, and I was wrapped up and taken away. She was taken to her room. I was taken somewhere. I'm sure we must have seen each other occasionally to try to breastfeed. Basically, she was in bed, and I was alone in the nursery—for ten days. All I know is that those ten days were the most horrible ten days of my life, terrifying beyond words. I had the feeling of being discarded, a horrible, bad piece of garbage, and of there being nothing good about me. I still can feel the terror in my body, right around my belly. I often feel pain and terror. I can remember it, very amazingly clearly, that feeling; it's so connected to me.

Lacking the intellectual ability to know and understand what is happening and caught in a web of confusion, fear, and pain, an infant often personalizes the experience and concludes that she is worthless or somehow to blame, that "something is terribly wrong with me." The cumulative impact of Donna's birth traumas led her to that conclusion. She felt it at a deep, unconscious level within her body. Why else wouldn't she be with her mother? Throughout the previous months, her mother had been not only her lifeline but also her entire world. But when she was separated immediately after birth, she thought, "Where am I? Everything familiar to me has disappeared. What is wrong? Was I bad?"

If the need for togetherness is not satisfied, the stress hormone ACTH continues to be produced, keeping the newborn in a continuous state of anxiety for an extended time. In cases of acute trauma, when the body and mind are flooded with too much pain to process, the system goes into a state of shock in order to survive. Such was the level of Donna's terror, rage, and pain that she went into shock.

Furthermore, she was learning to expect a cold, stark, inhospitable world of physical and emotional anxiety. As Liedloff has explained, "The infant in arms is in a state of bliss. The infant out of arms lives in a state of longing in the bleakness of an empty universe" (Liedloff, 1982).

Beliefs imprinted so early in times of extreme danger create patterns in the musculature and in the brain, where they remain and influence later reactions. Donna would later project her expectations and her fear out onto the world and respond to it accordingly.

Cellular biologist Bruce Lipton has said of the effects of traumas on the physical and mental health of the individual that "it is as if a master switch throws everything into a protective survival mode" (Lipton, 2005). After experiencing severe shock and neglect, a child may be permanently locked into hypervigilance. Fifty years later, Donna still lived with the belief that something was wrong with her.

Effects of Medication

Donna's mother did not recover quickly from the birth. She developed phlebitis in her legs and was given sulfa drugs (which were popular at the time) to counteract the inflammation. Donna recalled that

after ten days of terror, my mom was able to take me home, but she had been lying flat in bed for ten days. She was given sulfites to help the phlebitis, but she wasn't in very good shape. She was breastfeeding me, and the drugs were coming through her system and making me sick. I got terrible gas. I would just bloat up horribly every time I ate—and my father would have to walk around bouncing me on his shoulder.

Even today, I still have to be really careful about what I eat. I'm certain it was connected to the drugs my mother was taking, which I was getting from nursing. My whole immune system was compromised at that time. I had different kinds of illnesses as a baby…one thing after another.

Of her psychological state, Donna said,

We both ended up with a terrible fear of pain, anxiety, and discomfort. I just didn't feel safe. I did not feel safe with my mother, did not feel safe anywhere. It was terrifying and didn't stop being that way just because we got together again when we went home. Things with us had been so disrupted, so damaged on every level—physical, emotional, and spiritual—that making things okay was not easy.

My birth totally affected the entirety of my existence. I didn't feel safe any place, except maybe out in the trees or in nature at the beach. I could feel safe there for a little bit. But basically, I never felt safe and could not take in food or digest it, or I would eat and throw up. Every time I'd eat, I would get sick. I couldn't trust people or very few people. I might learn to trust them over a long period of time, but generally speaking, I don't trust human beings. I have a hard time doing anything in the world because it's just too scary. It's too hard. I get a stomachache…I've struggled with health problems all my life. I have to be very careful of what I eat. It's been an ongoing stress my whole life…I can't go anywhere without getting sick. I'm just afraid.

Donna became a sickly, difficult child and was a cause of concern and anxiety for her parents. Her own feelings of not being right were reinforced repeatedly by her "way of being in the world" with food, with people, and with herself. People saw her as a troubled child, and Donna was constantly reminded that something was wrong with her. In her own eyes, she became both "the problem, and the problem child."

School Years

Many factors, including the use of forceps, birth trauma, and early neglect or abuse can cause organic brain damage and impair cognitive abilities. We also know that a tense, frightened child who feels she doesn't have any intrinsic worth is likely to have difficulty learning and adjusting to a classroom environment.

It is not surprising that Donna had a very difficult time in school. Given her state of hypervigilance and possible early developmental brain damage, her scholastic skills were marginal. She also had difficulty paying attention in class.

In school, I had a really hard time learning to read. I know that I'm an intelligent person. I went to college, but I just couldn't learn the simple skills of reading and mathematics. So I ended up going to a special school.

I'd be embarrassed for people to know how little I can do with the basics. That side of my brain just doesn't work. The use of the forceps may have caused some kind of minimal brain damage; that's just on the physical level. But I also think it was the terror of not trusting, this level of not feeling organically safe in my body. I couldn't concentrate. I couldn't focus on all those things that they tried to teach me. I just felt they were further scary invasions of some kind, like they're trying to put stuff into my head. It's even hard for me now to listen to other people talk too much, to let things in. It seems like it was connected to feeling like the doctor was telling me when the right time to be born was. It just felt so invasive, so incredibly disrespectful, so absolutely, horrendously discounting. Then the forceps came in, and the pain created this sense that "letting in" is just not safe. Anything that teachers were going to try telling me, or anything at all, could be dangerous. Life's just not safe!

Like Donna, many people who were violently pulled out of the birth canal with forceps have an extreme sensitivity to anything perceived as invasive, either physically or psychologically. Donna's anxiety extended to her fear of teachers who might "put stuff into her."

In such cases, fear can extend to a distrust of all authorities and lead to an unwillingness or inability to cooperate. There is an unconscious need to protect oneself in the event "it" might happen again. When the awareness of what "it" was is forgotten or repressed, the fear and need to be on guard becomes habituated as a way of life.

Eventually, Donna's parents took her out of public school and enrolled her in a private school that was less focused on intellectual skills.

Adult Years as a Mother

Giving birth has the potential to restimulate a woman's unconscious and repressed messages about her own birth. If her birth was loving and easy, she is apt to approach the delivery of her babies with an underlying confidence and optimism.

Donna's memory of her birth was one of anger, fear, and pain, but when she in turn became pregnant, she attempted to give birth in as natural a way as possible, unconsciously trying to avoid what had occurred during her own birth. With her daughters, Donna was hoping to have what she had missed with her own mother.

Birth trauma, and lack of bonding, can severely blunt a child's willingness to trust and love his or her mother. (Of course, birth trauma and a lack of bonding are equally shattering to a woman who is desperate to establish a loving, warm relationship with her child but who realizes that she can't connect to her child.) Often, women who had no bonding experience with their own mother have an unconscious resistance to being vulnerable. This had been the situation between Donna and her mother for years.

Unfortunately, when it was Donna's time to give birth, many of the same mistakes were made and led to similar patterns for her daughters.

In the first photograph of my daughter, her eyes just looked terrified. They took a picture of my first baby when she'd just been born, and there is just sheer terror in her eyes, absolute terror. That's exactly how I felt [as an infant]. The exact same thing—but for her, the hospital stay was only two days instead of ten days. I didn't get phlebitis because I was a dancer, and I was up dancing the next minute. But it doesn't matter. There was still this sense of severance—total severance—and we've struggled. We can work on healing, but it has totally affected our whole relationship.

The opportunity for Donna to bond with her second daughter was disrupted even more.

When my second was born, she had a little something wrong with her nose, just a little closure at one place. They immediately whipped her off to the incubator. She was not premature. She was a ten-pound baby, but she had a little trouble with her breathing. I think two weeks in the incubator was a little exaggerated; it wasn't totally necessary. I stayed in the hospital for several days, but then I would go and visit her two or three times a day. I really needed to touch her; I really needed to take her out [of the incubator] more, but I wasn't allowed. I felt like the incubator separated us. She wasn't my baby anymore. They put her in this thing, and they encouraged me to connect.

I had tried to be much more enlightened the second time I gave birth. I did the Lamaze breathing. I was sure not to have a spinal. I didn't have any medication, basically, and she was very easy being born. But I never saw her face, and they never put her on my body to touch her. Now she can't breathe half the time. She has terrible breathing problems. She can't eat without having breathing problems. There's this layer of problems.

Again, mother and child were not given the time and support they needed or as Nature intended. History was repeating itself. Donna must have sensed it when she visited her daughter knowing she was not allowed to touch her. In such situations, when the innate desire for belonging is denied, it is not unusual for a woman to feel as if her baby does not belong to her.

Perhaps if Donna's daughter had spent those days after birth lying in her mother's arms, her difficulties with breathing would have lessened. Instead, she was alone in an incubator for two weeks. Like Donna at her own birth, she felt abandoned.

Donna's experience of giving birth to her third daughter was different.

I had a woman doctor with my third daughter. Two women were down at that end and men were up at my head. They actually kept my daughter in the room and put her on my body. So I felt connected to her. I made eye contact with her. She made eye contact with her father. It was profound. Then they took her away, but only for a day. They would bring her all wrapped up, and I would unwrap her. I went home as quickly as possible. That was as enlightened a birth as I could get at that time. I think because of what happened to me, I unconsciously was concerned and wanted to do it in a good way.

Looking at the effects of her daughters' births on their lives, Donna said this:

> My daughters' births have impacted them incredibly. My oldest daughter is afraid of her feelings, afraid to be vulnerable, afraid to feel. She has this beautiful heart. She is one of the most beautiful, loving beings, but she is afraid to feel. And if she goes away, she can't allow herself to miss anyone. It's too scary to know that you miss somebody. She can never say, "I miss you." She just has to close down. My second daughter has so much fear and anxiety. She's not sure of herself, not sure she's okay as a human being. She goes into shame and pain.

Early Trauma and PTSD

The fact that traumatic birth experiences like Donna's can generate PTSD in infants is only now being recognized. We know that early pre- and perinatal wounds are usually hidden from conscious memory, but that does not mean they are not active in our unconscious mind. Like a volcano, old pain may erupt at any time. As Bruce Lipton says, "The subconscious has all the data, and runs the show" (Lipton, 2005).

With PTSD, when the original terror is activated, the soldier, or in this case Donna, is overtaken by the horrific event. The individual is no longer in present time but in the hell of the past. Donna experienced a restimulation of the original trauma whenever she felt criticism or rejection; overcome with terror and crying uncontrollably, she would immediately regress to a screaming infant and curl into a fetal position in some corner.

Uncontrollable outbursts such as Donna's seem incomprehensible, but emotionally and psychologically, she was reliving her experience as an infant and the terror she felt as a newborn. She herself was baffled by her behavior.

> I didn't know…What could this be? Why am I feeling like I'm only a day old? I literally would feel that way—like I was a little baby. It was

a strange reenactment, and I was also ashamed of it. It was a total regression. It would come about from somebody saying something harsh or critical, and then zap! I'd be there, just crying like a little baby, but saying, "This is strange, this is odd, and this is really weird." But the pain, right in the stomach would be this pain, not just physical, but this—I don't know if I can describe it—like a physical and emotional pain. It is excruciating. There's nothing there, just pain in the heart, and in the stomach, and I couldn't come out of it. It might take three hours or more before I could just calm down enough to come out of it.

In episodes like these, once that switch is thrown, there isn't any reasoning or rational control. In the grip of primitive instincts, she had no way of stopping the episode. For Donna, the screaming and crying, and the pain and terror of those episodes, simply had to run their course. After three to four hours, she would eventually become exhausted and quiet. As her rational mind gradually returned, she would become aware of the outside world and painfully see the terror of her three young daughters. "Each one them as children also experienced the times I went into that terror."

Deeply affected by the frightening scenes they witness, young children record their panic and develop their own internal survival techniques. Never knowing when an outburst might occur or what might precipitate one, Donna's young daughters lived in a perpetual state of anxiety and stress.

I'd go to a therapist and talk about it, but the therapist didn't get it, didn't know what it was. Sometimes I'd feel too ashamed to tell anybody about it, because I didn't even know what it was. I couldn't talk about it. So nobody made any connection. And of course my husband thought I was sick and insane. The children were terrified too. They didn't know what was wrong. I was ashamed and terrified, too, not knowing what it was.

Healing Early Trauma

In *Waking the Tiger,* Peter A. Levine (1997), a researcher who has studied trauma in humans, wrote:

> The traumatized veteran, the rape survivor, the abused child…have been confronted by overwhelming situations. If they are unable to orient and choose between fight and flight, they will freeze or collapse…To move through trauma we need quietness, safety, and protection…We need support from friends and relatives, as well as from professionals. With that support and connection, we can begin to trust and honor the natural process that will bring us completion and wholeness, and eventually peace (p.35).

Like Levine, I believe that the symptoms of traumas hold "the very energies, potentials, and resources necessary for their transformation (Livine, 1997, p.3)" and I believe that traumas need to be experienced through the body and senses and brought into consciousness for true healing to occur. When past traumas become conscious, they can be dealt with in present time, and they lose their powerful hold on one's life. Levine (1997) has explained that:

> most trauma therapies address the mind through talk, and the molecules of the mind through drugs. Both of these approaches can be of use. However, trauma is not, will not, and can never be fully healed until we also address the essential role played by the body. We must understand how the body is affected by trauma and its central position in healing its aftermath (p.3).

This understanding is an essential element of trauma therapy.

Donna's "nursery terrors" were the instinctive efforts of her body to experience the trauma and heal itself. Yet the conscious awareness necessary to complete the healing process was missing, and because her trauma was not connected to its original source, no matter how much therapy she received, it remained unhealed.

Donna's work with me provided this missing part of the process. By regressing to the time of her birth, Donna was able to consciously re-experience her trauma.

Empowered by Knowledge

For Donna, the discovery of the impact of her birth and its role as the source of so many debilitating symptoms was life changing. This knowledge empowered her to make other choices in dealing with the nightmare in which she had lived. Those of us who work in the field of pre- and perinatal psychology know the powerful energy released in such transformational work. We have witnessed how previously lost potentials and resources emerge in our clients. Donna's simple, eloquent words reveal her healing process:

> After working on my birth, I have a lot more insight. I'm feeling peace and hope...that I'm unraveling what it is that happens. When I understand, I immediately can see the connection, and it releases. Now, I can make a different decision, such as not slipping there like I used to. I might still go into the same feelings for a little bit, but now I think about what's really happening. I don't have to think that all that pain is about what's happening in present time. I can take some of that power away from it. I have a moment and put it back to something in the past, and say, "Oh, that's what it is," and let it go a little bit. It lightens it. I might at first make the same hit, but I can release it. I don't have to stay in that dark hell. I can learn different ways of thinking about it and responding to it, and learn how to take care of myself and how to be with myself.
>
> Now I am remembering who I naturally am, who I was to begin with, before all this happened, which is the gift I do have. I do remember who I am. If I didn't remember my soul, my spirit, I'd really be in trouble. I'd be in an insane asylum, or I'd be on the street. I could not have been anything if I didn't have a connection with my spirit and parents who loved me.

Fortunately for Donna, her loving parents did not punish her for her problems. The patience and kindness shown by her mother and father helped to prevent her from making any disastrous, dangerous choices.

I was lucky that I didn't end up hurting someone. That was partly because of my parents and my own level of awareness and because I had therapists all the time. There was always somebody I could call. I was just lucky to not end up in a situation that would have been a zillion times worse. Then, I would have had no chance at all…put in an institution, given drugs, and then locked up. I would have gotten worse and worse. Of course, then my children would not have had any chance of ever thinking I was okay. Now, at least, I have a pretty good relationship with each one of them. I do what I can to be helpful and be someone they can respect, someone they can point to and say, "Wow, look, she's really working on her problems." I have the intention of really becoming the best I can: my whole self.

It may look like a small thing to start putting someone in ice cubes, but right now I'm shaking. Just the memory of it causes spells when I get cold and start shaking all over, my whole body. All through my life, I'd just start shaking intensely. I didn't know why. My body could never, never forget what happened. It's such a profound thing that I thought I was rejected by my mother, by God, by everything—everything that is of extreme value. When you are a spirit and you come here and you believe you've been discarded by God, your mother, and everything, what could you possibly think of yourself but that you're just a discard, a piece of garbage? Your instinct is to be born at the right time, to come out when you feel like it; I mean, the energy and feeling is "This is good, now I'm coming out. I'm a powerful, strong human being." Then I was stopped. "Nope, you are wrong. You are wrong!" Then came the ice, the drugs, the forceps.

I'm always hitting that wall, without any desire to do anything. [I think,] "No, might as well go back to sleep, forget that one, go into a coma, don't do that." That's basically the way I have lived ever since my birth. It's also been hard for me to ever go all the way through with any action, to complete anything.

It was so amazing to me to realize these things…just here and there, beginning to have a little bit of information. You can see that birth is underneath everything. Knowing opens whole worlds of understanding. You can do all kinds of therapy until you're blue in the face, and it may help a little, but it doesn't get at the core of the fear that's in your body. It's so basic that it affects your health, your life, and your attitudes, absolutely everything.

Before the ice cubes, my mother was fine. There was nothing wrong with her. There was nothing wrong with me. And then, everything was wrong! Everything was wrong forever and ever, it seems to me. They say that forever and ever is all that you have. I've been trying to fix it forever and ever.

The clearing and amazement Donna expresses is not unusual. In general, people do not believe that traumas before or during birth have any psychological significance. That it is possible to recall those very early experiences is even more unbelievable to some people. Clients are surprised at the relative ease of recovering those memories. But then they see that they actually live out early imprints daily in their lives. We all do.

It took years for Donna to escape from her birth trauma. It had followed her every day of her life. The few hours of respite she may have felt when she was out in nature were the exception, not the rule. The emotions and programmed reactions from her early wounds were always waiting in the wings, ready to spring onto the stage of her life whenever given the chance.

Also, typical of many infants who sustain pre- and perinatal damage, for many years Donna blamed her mother.

I was angry with her for forty years. I thought, "It's she who rejected me." I was scared. I was scared of her fear. I was angry with her because I felt she had thrown me away. She had abandoned me. She had discarded me, and I didn't know why, but I was mad. I was mad at her because I couldn't connect. I didn't know how, and she was scared, and I couldn't figure out what was wrong. I wanted to connect, but she seemed too scared. It was this disconnected feeling. I just couldn't figure out how to get through to her. Then I gave up, and I would get disdainful and cold and angry with her. Years later, when my mother died, I felt really bad that we had lost all that time. I began to realize that this wasn't something she had intentionally done to me, and she had suffered from it as much as I had. But I didn't learn that until years later.

Donna's story exemplifies the tragic emotional consequences of birth trauma and the separation of mother and child. They each wanted to love the other but could not find a way. For forty years, Donna saw her mother through the eyes of fear and anger. She found it very difficult to become vulnerable and to open her heart to her. Years were lost that could have brought them the friendship, joys, and love of a close mother-daughter relationship.

In addition, Donna's therapy hours were often spent processing problems with her mother. She was able to see her mother through the eyes of love only after focusing therapy work on her experience of birth. Sadly, that occurred late in her mother's life.

Like Donna, many people realize that their mothers were not the enemy only when they process early pre- and perinatal wounds. They see that their mothers had not chosen to cause them pain. As in Donna's case, often both the mother and the infant were helpless victims. With that awareness, years of strife can melt away, creating new opportunities to heal old wounds and relationships.

Brent

Brent, a computer programmer and talented woodworker, attended one of our STAR workshops with his wife. As a scientist trained in concrete proofs, he was rather dubious about the workshop, yet his creative, artistic side was open to the moment. He was curious about what he might discover and learn from this new experience.

Early on, he expressed an interest in regressing to his birth. Imagining he was in his mother's womb, he felt a strong, positive feeling of contact with her. "There was a feeling of unmitigated joy, ecstasy, and gratitude for being connected with her." He was ready to make his journey down the "birth canal" because he felt all was going well.

Suddenly, he felt "extreme anger and fear." Almost as quickly, he clutched up and kicked as if to defend himself. "I felt some sort of poison hit me." This feeling of "poison" hitting him, then his fear, anger, and retaliation, was repeated in several cycles. He said, "It came in waves." Then he began to fight. He felt something was wrong. "I was being held back! I began in earnest to fight to be born." He shouted, "Let me out! I will be born!" He felt hands holding him down and preventing his progress. After he was "out," he looked for his mother—he sensed she was near, and he would find her. He heard her voice again and returned to singing his birth song. He had a strong feeling that his father was not present.

After the regression, he wrote nine pages of detailed memories of the experience, his thoughts, and feelings. It took him by surprise. "The recollection seemed real and palpable. It felt as if it had actually happened." At no time had he heard the story of his birth. "I knew nothing about that day."

He wanted to know what his mother would say, so when he and his wife returned home from the workshop, he invited his mother to dinner. He was curious to hear her report of her pregnancy and his birth. He was careful not to lead her with specific questions, and her report "blew him away."

She had wanted a natural childbirth and taught herself the Lamaze breathing technique. She was a nonsmoker and also avoided alcohol during the pregnancy. She said I was very active in womb, so she would often use touch and motion to "respond to me." It's no wonder I felt unmitigated joy.

If these coincidences weren't enough, should it surprise me when my mother told me that the doctors were shouting at her to stop pushing and held her legs tightly together because I was a "threatened breech birth"? They finally had to anesthetize her to have the time they needed to turn me around. She was angry because that wasn't her original intention; plus, she was scared the drugs would affect me.

As a trained scientist, I could well imagine that one, two, or even three points could match, quite by accident. That's just probability.

But to have each and every major element of my regression experience and follow-up writing points match the actual birth experience—(1) mother and I communicated prior to birth; (2) the womb was a happy place; (3) later I felt anger, fear, and poison; (4) here was a serious difficulty; and (5) I felt held back—that presents a preponderance of evidence that would suggest "your body knows."

I was trained to doubt, to be skeptical of things that can't be measured. Relying solely on anecdotal tales would be cause for banishment from the society of scientific thinkers. But I am now firmly convinced that there is far more going on in our world—and our consciousness—than classical Western science would have us believe. Even at the very least, if I were to discount considerations of the collective or cosmic consciousness, there apparently is quite a bit here to suggest that we remember pre- and perinatal events at a deep, cellular level.

You can't really measure it—as far as I know—but it is most definitely there. You just need to stop thinking, close your eyes, and remember.

Summing Up

There is widespread international concern over the shared environment of the earth but too little concern over the ecology of the womb. Yet this universally experienced human environment may be the most important factor in ensuring the possibility of a peaceful future. Errors and damage at this most vulnerable time of development threaten the lives of our children. Their health, creativity, and productivity can be compromised.

Damage done in the womb or at birth can be corrected and lives can be redirected, but only if we recognize the source of the problem. We must recognize that addictions, psychoses, illnesses, and other chronic afflictions experienced by a pregnant woman may affect the developing fetal brain. The more severe and repetitive the stress, the more the individual's life will deviate from Nature's design and from its positive potential.

It is interesting to speculate what might have happened if Donna's mother had not gone to the hospital. Recall that the baby was coming out quickly! Had Donna been born at home, there would not have been any disruption or violent interventions. After birth, her mother would have held Donna, and the bond of trust and connection would have continued. She and her mother would not have been terrified. Furthermore, without mandatory hospital bed rest, it is unlikely her mother would have developed phlebitis, so there would not have been any sulfa drugs to cause the baby digestive problems and weaken her system. What would Donna's life have looked like without the trauma and shock of ice cubes, forceps, isolation, and illness? It might have been far different from what Donna experienced at home, in school, in social situations, and later as a mother.

No doubt putting a laboring woman and her infant in an ice cube bath would not happen today. We are more aware and sensitive to babies in the womb and the fact that they are conscious and responding to their environment. We now recognize the critical importance of honoring the time right after birth for mother-infant bonding. We now know that when biological needs for togetherness and affirmation are not met, a child may search endlessly for ways to satisfy them, looking to fill the hole where mother's love should have been.

However, many of the clients that therapists see today were born in earlier days, without the benefit of enlightened medical practices, state-of-the-art neonatal intensive care units, and conscious, committed providers; they were born in an age when babies were routinely taken away from their mothers after birth. Women were told, "You need rest. We will take your baby to the nursery and bring her back later" (at the staff's convenience). This is one reason why therapists need to include and explore pre- and perinatal experiences, where they may uncover the roots of hidden trauma. The body remembers. The unconscious knows.

We have made great strides toward following Nature's plan. We believe it will make a difference. As we look forward to better outcomes and happier children, we must also do what we can to free clients from the results of trauma in their past.

Francis Bacon once said, "The only way to control Nature is by obeying her" (Bacon, 2012, p.34). We must ensure that our current practices do not disobey her.

The simple act of taking babies away from their mothers and isolating them from their mothers' beating heart and warming touch can contribute to years of living without trust, without our unfettered hearts, and without the accompanying innermost, essential spiritual awareness, which is the legacy of our Divine Creator. When you add deeds of separation, violent births, unwanted babies, child abuse, and psychological abuse, the cost to us individually and as a society is staggering.

6

When the Bough Breaks:
Separation at Birth

Hush a bye, baby, on the tree top,
When the wind blows the cradle will rock;
When the bough breaks, the cradle will fall,
And down will come baby, cradle and all.

Mother Goose's Melody, ca. 1765

Nature has built-in biological programs and expectations to ensure a safe transition from within the womb. The newborn infant, whose world has been his mother's body, belongs in his mother's arms immediately after birth. This is because babies are not fully developed at birth. They require more time and further protection in the arms of a safe, loving human being, ideally the mother, for an optimal outcome. The key words are *safe* and *loving*.

If instead a newborn is separated from his mother after birth, there is a disruption in Nature's design. The classic nursery rhyme "Rock-a-bye Baby" is a metaphor for what happens to a baby when the programmed support system is broken and the mother vanishes. "Down will come baby, cradle and all." In the case of unavoidable separations from the mother due to medical emergencies, it is helpful if the father, or another close family member, is there to hold and cradle the child.

Whatever the reason for the emergency that separates the mother and child, the emergency and the separation are frightening for the baby, and if the baby is experiencing fear, normal development must pause while protective systems are activated. As cellular biologist Bruce Lipton explains, "Cells can grow and develop or they can protect themselves. They can only do one or the other" (Lipton, 2005, p.3).

Hopefully, it will be a short time before the baby is returned to safe, loving arms. However, as Bruce Perry (2007) notes, when the separation lasts for an extended time, "the brain will reset, acting as if the individual is under persistent threat." "Down will come baby," as the brain moves into a protective response and the individual assumes a constant vigilance. Developmental opportunities as well as the potential for healing, intimate relationships, and other vital lessons in life will be lost. The psychological damage may be slight or catastrophic, but trauma will be recorded biologically in the cellular structure of the child. It will be filed away in the unconscious.

These early biological impressions of the trauma embedded in the cellular structure of the body and in the myelin-covered pathways forming in the developing brain cannot be easily erased. Contrary to prevalent belief, the infant will not just snap back and forget. Babies are not malleable, and their bodies remember.

The most tragic separation that can happen at birth is the death of either the mother or the baby. When the baby dies, the deeply painful loss is recognized and followed by a long period of mourning. The baby's death is heartbreaking for everyone involved, including parents, extended family and friends, and medical personnel. Compassionate support is usually given, especially to the grieving parents.

In contrast, when the mother dies, while there is sympathy for the "poor little baby," there is scant recognition of the depth of the infant's grief or of his need to be comforted and to mourn his loss. Our society does not readily perceive the fetus or newly born child as a conscious, feeling, and learning creature, and the psychological implications of pre- and perinatal trauma are often ignored, made light of, or denied.

It is important to understand that birth is on a continuum with life in the womb. Research that supports prenatal consciousness shows that babies are aware, conscious, and learning, even before birth (Chamberlain, 1998). According to Thomas Verny (1981), author of *The Secret Life of the Unborn Child*, "The fetus can see, hear, experience, taste, and on a primitive level, even learn in utero. Most importantly, he can feel—not with an adult's sophistication, but feel nonetheless" (p.12).

The infant knows his connection with his mother has broken. "When the bough breaks," the infant is torn away from all he has known. The baby, who has been cradled in the familiar body and mind of his mother, descends into despair.

Those of us dedicated to the field of pre- and perinatal psychology understand that traumatized infants, including those who have lost their mothers, may later suffer from PTSD. The infants may be labeled by other names and called "fussy" or "irritable." As children, they may be diagnosed as hyperactive or as having attention deficit disorder. (In those cases, the focus is on the symptoms, instead of the cause.)

Does separation from a mother as a baby mean the child will be damaged permanently? No. There are ways to heal the broken bond, or even to build a new one if no bond has been established. Fortunately, the degree of the trauma can be ameliorated by the consistency and quality of subsequent care given to the baby, and the potential of this care must never be underestimated.

The earlier help is given, the easier it is to correct unhealthy patterns and prevent further harm. But without early intervention, personality defenses are formed and habituated over time. Eventually, they can become second nature. Attitudes and behaviors are then developed to support those defenses, as can be seen in the following story.

Beth

Beth was only sixteen when I met her. Born via an emergency C-section as her mother was dying, Beth was ushered into life in a confluence of death and birth. No plans had been made for this situation. Beth's father was ill-equipped to be a mother to his baby, and everything was in a state of chaos. Under the stress, her father did all he could to take care of his motherless daughter. He took a few weeks off to deal with the situation and was able to find daycare placements, babysitters, and a string of surrogate mothers to help take care of Beth when he was at work. Beth said, "I do have some fuzzy but good memories of the woman who lived catty-corner to our house. My maternal grandmother lived in the area and actually, all through elementary school, I stayed at her house after school."

When Beth was seven, her father remarried and had another child, a son who was the apple of his mother's eye. The new baby boy was pampered, given more Christmas presents, and could do no wrong. In contrast, in the eyes of her stepmother, Beth, who was known as being "difficult," could do no right.

The situation then became worse for Beth. She felt she was being excluded and continually felt unwanted. Without anyone to talk to about her feelings or any way to process her anguish and problems or what she perceived was happening, she acted out her feelings in her behavior with food. She began stealing and hiding food and routinely "stuffed the food down" her fragile frame. She needed food to help her cope.

In time, her relationship with her stepmother became so strained that Beth was sent to live with a foster family. Again, she felt "cast out" and abandoned—alone with no one who really cared about her. It was not the first or the last time that she would feel that way.

Eventually, Beth went to live with new foster parents whose home was nearby her school. But during the years that she lived in the care of the kindly older couple, her acting-out behaviors escalated. Many of her problems continued to be centered on food. She compulsively hoarded it, stockpiling heaps under beds or in drawers and closets, as if hiding it away for some future need. The hidden food would spoil and smell, creating an unpleasant problem for her caretakers. She lied to cover up the source of the odor and the location of her stashes, and she was filled with shame and anguish as she struggled for ways to understand and explain her "weird behavior." She could not stop.

When describing that period of her life to me, her voice fell to a painful moan as she whispered to me, "I was afraid I could never have enough. I thought I had to hide. I had to store it. I had to fill something in me that was very empty."

Beth was having difficulties in school, both academically and socially. Her foster parents were aging and decided they could no longer care for her. Since they had been good to Beth, and she did not want to leave them, their decision to retire precipitated the critical situation that brought Beth to therapy. She was in a crisis. Her stepmother would not allow her to return to her father's home. Meanwhile, her father was worried about where his daughter would live and found her an apartment. He was also concerned about who would make time for her and who would offer her advice on the challenges facing her, a sixteen-year-old living on her own.

Her father's therapist was aware of Beth's history and suspected that the trauma around her birth might be the source of her difficulties. The therapist was correct. She also knew that one of the few therapy programs that address pre- and perinatal issues was my program, STAR. For over a quarter century, we had pioneered innovative and powerful methods of working with the wounds of birth traumas.

The therapist was confident that the best environment for dealing with such early pain was in a safe residential setting. Beth's father made arrangements to consult with me, and we agreed to accept Beth into the STAR program. When she arrived at our Pocket Ranch sanctuary in California, she was scared, but she hoped she would find answers and relief from her suffering.

Therapy at STAR

During her time at STAR, Beth worked on many issues in her life, including difficulties with her stepmother, her father, and her problems with food. As she peeled back the layers of her defenses and began to feel safe and cared for, she talked about her birth and the death of her mother. She risked being vulnerable and open about her issues with food and said she wanted to explore her birth.

Eventually, in one session, she regressed back to her deepest trauma, her birth and the loss of her mother. She felt an overwhelming panic. She felt she was dying and that there was no possible way she could get what she wanted and needed to survive. Her fear was palpable. She felt helpless and alone in a life-and-death situation. She was desperately struggling for breath and a way to get out of her dying mother. "I'm dying," she cried out, "I'm dying."

In fact, she had almost died. When the surgeon cut into the womb, he found a tiny blue baby girl with the umbilical cord wrapped around her neck, depriving her of oxygen. A few minutes later, her mother died.

Years later, to ward off the terror and the possibility of death, Beth compulsively squirreled away food and overate to ensure she would have enough. At a deep, primitive level, she was warding off death over and over again. She was also trying to stuff down her fear and her deep, piercing grief—the grief (that feeling of emptiness) that no one, not even Beth, could fully acknowledge.

At the end of the regression, sobs shook her body as she lay curled up holding herself. Her grief was finally being released. She was touching upon the depth of her empty yearning for her mother, and this time she was not alone. Someone was with her to offer support and comfort.

As she and I continued to explore the issues around her birth, threads from her mother's history emerged—they, too, had been woven into Beth's experience. As the work of Dr. Myriam Szejer, a child psychiatrist and psychoanalyst in Paris who "communicates" with newborns facing life and death crises, reminds us, we are not separate from our families' histories. Szejer, who is president of La Causes des Bébés, investigates the mother's history and the story of her pregnancy, including all the factors that may cause failure to thrive. She believes that telling the story to the newborn can improve the outcome for the infant, and her work has been so valuable that hospitals call on her remarkable skills when a newborn is struggling.

In *Talking to Babies*, Szejer (2005) wrote, "The unconscious of the infant is totally open after birth. Therefore, what is being said and what is happening is taken in and recorded. It will later be repressed by the conscious mind but retained in the unconscious" (p.14). The eminent pediatrician Marshall Klaus, one of the world's experts on the importance of the mother-infant connection and the power of words spoken with a newborn present, agrees. In his 2005 DVD, *The Psychology of Birth*, he stated "This is a sensitive period for the mother and baby, and our words have great power. These babies are listening and recording every word."

Beth needed to recover a sense of what she had heard at birth and just after and retained in her unconscious.

Finding Clarity through her Mother's History

When Anne, Beth's mother, was born, her father wrote his infant daughter a letter. In it he said, "Oh, well, here you are. I don't want you, but I have to deal with you." Clearly, he was not happy to be a father.

He was so manipulative and abusive that Anne's mother divorced him and took two-year-old Anne with her when she left. Anne's mother never remarried and as a single mom did her best to raise her only child. She kept the malicious letter for many years and eventually gave it to her daughter.

Even though Anne's father never showed any tender concern, he did keep in touch with his daughter throughout the years. Beth said, "He used money to manipulate her into seeing him. In all the letters written to her, he was very abusive, playing with her mind, and putting her down in a very controlling way."

When he found out his daughter had married and was pregnant, he wrote another benchmark epistle. In his usual critical and attacking manner, he formally disowned her.

Anne received this final rejection from her father when she was nine months pregnant. She fell into a deep suicidal depression, and within days, went into labor. The accumulation of years of abuse and rejection from her father, which had started at her own birth, overwhelmed her.

It is not hard to imagine the angst Anne felt that so devastated her. Her father had repeatedly rejected her since her birth. This final blow came at a time that should have been joyful anticipation. Instead, it was one of great vulnerability and emotional pain. As Anne's friends later told Beth, Anne felt there was not enough space in the world for her and her father. During that last agonizing week, she said to several of her friends, "One of us has to go."

Lipton (2005) has explained that "the mother's belief about her environment is relayed to the fetus. If she sees a threatening environment, the fetus receives that perception." Anne's body and mind had been Beth's world as an unborn child, and Anne's understanding of life had been conveyed to Beth in the womb. Beth's world—through her mother—was filled with sadness, despair, parental rejection, and suicidal ideation. These perceptions were imprinted in Beth's open, undefended, and unconscious brain.

Making Connections

In therapy, Beth was finding threads of her history, connecting those to her mother's history, and beginning to make connections between her birth and her hoarding behaviors, yet she wanted more clarity.

Her father informed her that the doctor who had delivered her lived in a city close to the ranch. Arrangements were made for Beth and her father to visit this physician. It turned out that the doctor remembered her mother vividly. He quietly said, "Your mother was the only mother I ever lost."

He showed her a dream catcher in his office and shared with her that it was her mother who had made it and given it to him. Beth said, "The doctor told me she had come into the hospital in labor, and then it had simply stopped. They were unsuccessful at all their attempts to start labor again, and there were signs of fetal distress." An emergency C-section quickly followed. They discovered the umbilical cord was wrapped around Beth's neck twice—she was clearly being deprived of oxygen— but she was still alive. Nurses immediately attended to Beth, as the other medical staff desperately tried to save Anne's life. Anne remained unresponsive and several minutes later died.

Beth's life changed forever, and she was left with an aching emptiness. There were no warm arms for Beth. She heard no cooing, loving sounds from her mother. She never would. She had fallen with the cradle from the treetop, and her mother was not there to catch her. Her connection to all she had known was abruptly severed.

She was also in a state of oxygen deprivation when she was cut out of her mother's body. In shock from her brush with death and the sudden loss of her mother, Beth felt she was not safe; she felt she must find sustenance and prepare for imminent disaster. Lacking reassurance, she remained in a perpetual state of anxiety, need, and fear. Her mourning went underground.

Later, she became a rock: she shut down and built a shield around herself. She told me, "I am strong; nothing gets me, you know. I'm a survivor." She lived on her own private island, isolated from others, and hid food away in secret places.

Driven by her unconscious fear and compulsion to have enough, Beth made sure she would survive! She hid food for some future emergency, "just in case." There was no apparent logic to her compulsive behavior. However, seen through the eyes of a terrified, motherless infant, her defenses were logical. Her acting-out behaviors were survival strategies that made sense.

As a result of talking to the doctor, Beth began to understand what really happened to her mother and began to forgive herself and release the isolating guilt she had borne all her life. She realized her story was not just about herself. It included the legacy from her mother's sad history with her mean-spirited father.

> In therapy, I began to learn more about what happened with my mother's death, and I began to piece things together that had been a mystery for a long time. All that I had been told all my life was that mother just died. You don't just die. Something happened there. The only thing I knew of the story was that I had been born, so I thought it must have been this hard birth that killed her—that I had killed her.
> Now I realize I couldn't possibly have been to blame for her death. Things were going on that I had no control over. The burden of guilt that I have felt, that I had somehow caused her death, was lifted.

Beth later contacted several of her mother's friends who confirmed her mother's state of mind after she received her father's letter. Beth began to see how painful it was for her mother to be shut out of her father's life. The power of parental rejection is deep and painful—it was never far beneath the surface of Anne's consciousness. The rejection became a ghost that haunted all her other relationships. Even the approaching birth of her own child did not have the power to erase it from her mind. Beth concluded, "I think she just gave up in the middle of labor and started to slip away. She died a few minutes later, after I was born."

Losing her mother left Beth with feelings of emptiness, guilt, and insufficiency. Her sense of herself was very negative. But fortified with her newfound awareness, Beth was determined to not repeat her mother's script, even though her grandfather was still in her life.

Beth dealt with other issues in therapy, but the prism through which she viewed herself and life was built upon the trauma of her birth, and her chronic problems about food and eating were a part of the equation.

From therapy, I got a lot of insight into why I was eating to fill the void inside of me. So I have to hide it, store it, and fill something in me that is very empty. I've confronted my issues with food and the fear of never having enough.

The mother is the infant's source of food, prenatally as well as postnatally. Thus, that insatiable, empty place in Beth had a strong connection with the loss of her mother. Her ravenous and repressed biological and emotional needs for her mother had never gone away. They drove Beth to compulsively fill the bottomless hole that ached within her. It was not just food that she missed, it was her mother, and it was nurturing safety.

In therapy, she mourned and grieved that loss. Since then, she has gradually learned to deal more effectively with her addiction around food and to make healthier choices for herself.

From Fear to Love

If Beth had not dealt with her birth trauma, she would still be caught in the drama. It was part of her history, imprinted in her subconscious mind, and when the lessons of history are not learned, they are repeated over and over again into the next generation.

Beth was lucky. She was still in her teens when she did this work. With time, Beth was able to embrace her innocence.

I began to discover truth. I began to discover that I wasn't responsible for her death. There was no way that I could have caused it. With that realization, I could move on with my life. I began living my life. The therapy was a jumping-off point for me to start growing. I had been eating to fill the void in me.

This lovely, intelligent young woman has now graduated from college. As a student, she volunteered many hours to help underprivileged girls. She is very empathetic with the youngsters and wants some day to have a career working with young children.

She told me about a day when she saw a child playing outside all by himself. It was January and cold. He wore only a thin shirt and shorts. "He saw me, and his face lit up. He ran towards us, and grabbed me, and said, 'Take me home with you.' That just rips your heart out." Beth knows. She can relate.

She is compassionate and protective of the children in the childcare centers where she volunteers. Her feelings about the quality of care these youngsters receive are very strong. One day, she hopes to have her own children and be for them the mother she never had. She understands what is needed and feels she will be able to provide that level of care. She has clarity and self-understanding, which frees her.

> I have lots of freedom from not having to carry around that guilt. I have been able to open up to people more, to trust people more, to make friendships, and have healthier relationships. I'm not stuck in the past.

Beth's shift from fear to love represents the power of transforming old patterns. She inspires us to see it is possible for anyone with courage to take time and look within. It also brings us awareness of how painful it is for a baby to lose her mother. When Beth had her mother, there was no need to become an "island."

Summing Up

Mental health clinics and centers are filled with adults who have been severely harmed by events around their births. As in many cases of prenatal injuries, a cluster of events can cause trauma. Often, those very early wounds are not recognized; however, symptoms abound, ranging from severe depression to rage and schizophrenia, and are acted out in a myriad of ways throughout life. As Candace Pert (1999) said, "Such [early] trauma can profoundly affect later patterns of behavior."

The bough of nurturing care is surely severed when a baby's mother dies. Like lambs who, when they have lost their mothers, bleat and refuse food and even, when force-fed, waste away and die, the infant suffers a shattering loss that does not pass by without consequences. Even if death is not an outcome, without positive, consistent care and regard from the mother or a mother figure, babies feel anxious, afraid, lost, or angry.

In Beth's case, when the bough snapped, Beth was plummeted into a pattern of chronic loss and fear that shadowed her life and robbed her of the spontaneity and happiness of a free childhood.

Unfortunately, it is very common for the abandoned, neglected, or abused child, even at the earliest stages, to take on the blame for what happened. It is almost a given for a child who loses his mother to see himself as unworthy or at fault. Common refrains include "If I had been good, she wouldn't have given me away," "It was my fault she died," and "I'm basically not lovable, or she would not have left me." Lipton (2005) has stated, "These are the words that fit the individual—they are the lyrics that fit the underlying music." Such lyrics are also strongly influenced by the words spoken by people around the baby at the time, as Klaus (2001) has indicated. Those words also become the beliefs individuals who have lost their mothers have about themselves.

Researchers in brain development and psychoneuro- immunology confirm what many infants like Beth have experienced. A mother's death is a devastating loss and is experienced as a life-threatening event to the baby. When it occurs late in pregnancy or during birth, it becomes an emergency for all those involved, including the infant, whose unconscious is totally open after birth.[11] What words or meanings reached Beth's open state of consciousness? In that last week, what was she experiencing as her mother went into the deep depression that led to her death? From Beth's therapy work, we learned that it was absolute terror.

In the best of circumstances, a family member who will be in the child's life is there to take the newborn into her arms, holding, soothing, and gazing lovingly into the eyes of the traumatized baby. This scenario is more likely to occur in a less technologically advanced society, where family members, especially women, are present at births. In this family-centered event, women present at the birth are likely to remain in the life of the baby.

Losses other than the death of the mother in childbirth may cause the cradle to fall, propelling the baby into a lifetime of yearning for that lost object of love and care. The mother may be in jail or have her baby taken from her. Or the mother may have chosen to relinquish her baby for adoption. The scenarios are endless.

To prevent the trauma of separation no matter what the cause, we must do all we can to support Nature's bond of mother and infant. The word *cradle* in the Mother Goose melody of "Rock-a-Bye Baby" refers to "the earliest period of one's life" and "the place of one's origin." The verse quoted at the beginning of this chapter is traditionally known as a lullaby to encourage a baby to sleep. Perhaps it is also a warning. When we interfere with the cradle of life and cause it to fall, we are influencing the future development of the individual.

The mother is the cradle. When infants are deprived of their mothers or another loving surrogate at the beginning stages of life, they veer from their full potential. When the cradle falls, the baby's well-being also takes a tumble.

We must do all we can to support Nature's intention for mother and baby to be together, and we must intervene when that bond is broken. A loving caregiver who steps in during the mother's absence or death must also preserve this bond. Furthermore, in an attempt to "protect" children from loss, we must not disallow their ability to integrate loss; doing so would leave them with a larger, unhealed, festering wound (Klaus, 2001).

Through therapy focused on Beth's experience of birth, the shadows were lifted from Beth's mind and heart. Compulsive, unconscious needs to fill the past emptiness within her were replaced with a sense of herself and confidence in her future. She is building herself a cradle.

7

Heartbreak:

When a Baby Dies

There are only two or three human stories, and they go on repeating themselves
as fiercely as if they had never happened before.

WILLA CATHER, *O Pioneers!*

Several years ago at an Association for Prenatal and Perinatal Psychology
and Health conference in Amherst, Massachusetts, I attended a lecture
given by Australian neonatologist Dr. Peter Barr (1989), also a co-
producer with his wife, Deborah de Wilde, and psychologist Julie
Dunsmore, of the award-winning documentary film *Some Babies Die*. I was
very moved by his presentation. He spoke with great compassion and
wisdom about what happens when a baby dies. From my extensive notes,
these words stood out: "When a baby has died, he remains part of a
family, and he needs to be acknowledged, accepted, and experienced.
Too often, the infant body is hastily disposed of."

Dr. Barr's words acknowledged the depth of the trauma that occurs
when a baby dies. In contrast, the cheerful platitude "Oh, you can get
pregnant again, you'll be fine" only skims the surface and indicates the
speaker does not understand the enormity of the moment and the pain
involved. In fact, it is heartbreaking when a mother knows she is carrying

a dead baby within her womb; it is equally heartbreaking when she gives birth to a dead baby or watches her child die at birth or soon after. These events are as traumatic as going through a long, painful birth that threatens a mother's life. In each case, the effects of the trauma remain and haunt the consciousness of everyone involved, especially the consciousness of the mother.

Dr. Barr's words also pointed to the need to fully grieve a loss that will leave its mark on the family forever. Healing occurs when the parents of a baby who has died take time to lovingly hold the baby, give the infant a name, and acknowledge the brief life with a ceremony and a grave. If instead the experience of the infant's death is repressed or denied, there is a danger that emotions and memories may resurface and shadow the family members as well as the mother's next pregnancy and the babies born of her future pregnancies.

The following stories describe several individuals' experiences of the shadow cast over their lives and their families by the early death of an infant. Two of the stories involve the death of infants at or near birth and show how the painful tragedies threaded their way into the future. The first story shows how a mother's grief and fear triggered by the death of her first baby compulsively dictated her unhealthy treatment of a second child born years later. In the second story, the baby's death was quietly dealt with and on the surface "forgotten." It was too painful to talk about, so it was hidden in some corner of the mind. But it was not lost. It surfaced rather mysteriously decades later. The third story shows an enlightened way to deal with the death of a baby. The fourth story shows a process of healing that occurs years later.

Jacob

Jacob's mother had the great misfortune to be held in a Nazi concentration camp during World War II. In total helplessness and unable to find food for her baby, she held him day and night and watched him starve to death. She survived in spite of all the pain and trauma of the experience, but she would never forget the agony of watching her baby die in her arms. Unfortunately, at the time, there was no opportunity to follow her religious traditions and grieve her loss. Like an unhealed wound, the painful experience festered in her unconsciousness. Her baby died, the body was taken away—end of story. But there was no healing closure for her.

Several years after the camp was liberated, she married and immigrated to the United States and began to put together the pieces of her life. Fairly soon, she found out she was pregnant. When she gave birth to her second child, Jacob, the terror of the starvation and death of her first child was still alive in her consciousness. Her daily concern was the survival of her new baby. She became obsessive with feeding Jacob and compulsively overfed him. He became so overweight that he could no longer move about freely to navigate his world. Driven by her unconscious trauma in the concentration camp, she overfed him to make sure that the original tragedy would not be repeated. Jacob was a surrogate caught in the psychological web of his mother's earlier trauma. He became the fat kid and was teased and shunned throughout his school days.

Fortunately, in time, Jacob was able to disentangle from his mother's devastating history and now lives life as a healthy and successful psychologist.

Rachel

A professional woman originally from Missouri and residing in Georgia, Rachel came to one of my twenty-one-day STAR workshops. Early in the session when she was in a regressed state, she found herself in deep grief. She later told me that during the regression, she received a message from a brother who had died before she was born, a brother she had never seen and who was never talked about.

Here is what she wrote about the experience.

In my birth regression, my brother, the first of three children, who died the day after he was born, came into my mind. He told me the name he chose for himself, Jonathan David. He was telling me because no one else in the family was willing to acknowledge him, and he felt I would. He felt "unwitnessed." Our mother never even saw him.

After a difficult birth with abruptio placenta, there was massive hemorrhaging and an emergency C-section. The tiny infant died the next day. His father quickly took the body to the cemetery and had the remains buried while his wife was in the hospital recovering. There was no time or perceived need for any of the healing actions suggested in Dr. Barr's lecture. The newly born baby's body was "hastily disposed of," buried without a headstone or marker in his father's family plot and never mentioned again. However, the baby's death sent ripples through the family. Rachel's maternal aunt was pregnant about the same time, and she was traumatized by what had occurred to her sister. She miscarried her baby and vowed to never become pregnant again, even though her husband badly wanted a family. Their opposing views on this topic had major ramifications on their marriage.

A year later, Rachel's mother successfully gave birth to another son, who she named George M. Jones—the same name she had given the baby who died, a fact that came as a major shock to the living George when he accidentally learned of it sixty years later.

In therapy, Rachel cried over the death of her brother and grieved the absence of any recognition of his life as part of the family; it was as though he had never existed. Perhaps she was picking up the repressed grief and pain of her mother, who must have been so overwhelmed by the memory of her first child's death that she wanted to wipe it out of her mind. Perhaps at Rachel's birth, Rachel's consciousness was open to her mother's history, and Rachel took in everything that had happened to her mother and recorded it, but retained a knowledge of it only in her unconscious.

Rachel's regression experience was so profound for her that she felt she had to do something to affirm her baby brother's life, as brief as it was, to make real his place in the family. To find the first George's burial location, Rachel contacted the cemetery and spoke with the caretaker. She received the record of where the baby boy was buried and ordered a baby's breath shrub to be planted there. A few days later, unknown to her mother, she and her partner drove the distance from her home in Georgia to the cemetery in Missouri. In a quiet, intimate ceremony, Rachel introduced Jonathan David to two members of his family and honored the reality of his life. Later, she called her mother and told her what they had done. To her surprise, her mother seemed truly pleased to hear Rachel's report and said she was going to drive out to the cemetery right away to visit the gravesite. This was very healing for Rachel and must have been for her mother, too.

That was the only time Rachel heard her mother mention the baby she lost. In spite of Rachel's urging, her mother refused to talk about him, even to her second son, who shared the baby's name.

Her mother had had no bonding experience with the baby before he died, and she and Rachel's father had never healed their grief or had any closure for the death of their baby. Instead, there was repression and denial, which lasted for years.

Karen

Karen and her husband had a two-year-old daughter and were looking forward to having another child. About eight weeks into her second pregnancy, Karen, a physician's assistant specializing in women's health, suspected something was not right when her morning sickness stopped and she felt too good to be pregnant. A week later, a sonogram confirmed that the fetus was no longer alive: there was no heartbeat.

With her medical background, Karen knew that her pregnancy was high risk because she was thirty-eight years old. She also knew that a spontaneous abortion is a natural process if there is any irregularity in the development of the child. It's now known that most miscarriages (80%) pass on their own within two weeks, and the standard care now is to wait. If the patient doesn't want to wait, doctors recommend the use of vaginal misiprostil tablets to dilate the cervix, but they rarely do a D and C (Dilation and Curettage) procedure anymore because those are too traumatic to the uterus.

Karen chose not to have a D and C, but to let the fetus follow its natural process and come out in its own time. Two and a half weeks passed until this happened, during which time she mourned the remnants of a child within her. It is always hard to lose a baby, especially if your time is limited and you do not know if you will be able to conceive again.

When the fetus finally passed out of her body, it was tiny, still inside its sac, about the size of a walnut, but it had been the beginning of a life. Karen said goodbye to it and buried it beneath a favorite rose bush she had planted. She did this alone. It was an inner process for her, not something she wanted to talk about.

In about six months, she was pregnant again, and after a fairly easy pregnancy and delivery, she and her husband had another full-term, healthy little girl. Because of the effective, timely way she handled her earlier loss—she grieved and healed her grief then; she did not stuff it away and add fearful thoughts to carry and project onto the future—she did not have lingering negative effects.

Marylou

Marylou was a professional woman in her forties when she came to see me for therapy. She told me that earlier in her life, she had been in a relationship with a man named Ralph and had become pregnant. But Ralph felt it was too soon for them to become parents. He was sure about it and urged her to have an abortion. She had mixed feelings, but after thinking about it, she agreed. She was in her last year of law school. The timing was not right for her to become a mother. Maybe later, when she had a job in a good law firm making "good money," she would consider it. Besides she had some doubts about Ralph. So she had an abortion. It was "no big deal," and she went forward with her life. The relationship with Ralph continued with some great times and some bad ones. "Just like all relationships," she told me.

Several years later, she became pregnant again. It was a good time. Marylou was in her late thirties, and it felt like it was now or never. She and Ralph were both earning "good money" and in successful careers. She was excited about it, and though Ralph was not, he reluctantly agreed to support her desire to have a baby.

The pregnancy went well, but the birth was a nightmare. Contractions started late in the seventh month when she was in court working on an important case with her boss. Her water broke. She was in pain and mostly aware of her deep "pain and embarrassment." What a terrible time to go into labor. It was also too early. She fled the scene, called the doctor, and hailed a cab to get to the hospital as quickly as possible. The baby was coming! She called Ralph, but he was out of town on business and could not fly back that day.

The doctor came right away. He decided the baby was in a difficult position, and a C-section was performed. Marylou said, "I was so afraid something was wrong with the baby. It was a boy, a tiny boy, but he was beautiful and breathing. They let me see him and then rushed him off to Infant Critical Care and put him in an incubator. I was so tired and so relieved that I started to cry. It all happened so fast that I didn't have time to call my family. They took me to my room. I was so groggy and tired I fell asleep and slept all night long."

Marylou's sister and mother came the next day. They were not allowed in the ICU, but they could see the little baby boy in the incubator. Ralph returned and took Marylou home. She vowed to return to the hospital every day to see her little baby, Alan.

There were a lot of things she needed to do. She really wasn't ready. She hadn't gotten all the things a baby would need or found a capable and trustworthy baby nurse to take care of her baby when she went to work. She had to go to the office to deal with many legal matters she had on her work calendar. It was a hassle to get to the hospital every day, but she managed to and was falling in love with her baby. Soon she could hold him every day. The nurses were kind and answered her questions.

She accomplished all she had to do both at her office and home, including buying a beautiful white crib and everything else a baby might need. She hired an experienced, well-recommended baby nurse named Maude. By the time Alan was judged big enough to go home, Marylou was ready.

"I was so thrilled to finally bring <u>my</u> baby home," she told me. "My mother bought me a lovely rocking chair. We both loved rocking in it. A routine was established. The baby was a little fussy but slowly gaining weight. So I didn't worry. Nurse Maude knew exactly what to do. Ralph came by to see us and spent the weekends with us. Maude came every weekday before I had to go to work. I hated leaving my precious baby, but I knew he was in safe hands."

It must be one of the most shattering experiences a mother can have to tiptoe into the nursery to check on her baby and notice that he does not seem to be breathing. The horror Marylou must have felt.

Ralph was spending the night and heard her scream "No, no, no!" and came running. Marylou was trying to resuscitate little Alan. Ralph called 911 for an ambulance. It could not be true.

Marylou continued screaming hysterically, crying and holding the baby tightly to her breasts.

When the ambulance arrived and the attendants came into the bedroom, they confirmed that the baby had died. "Sorry," they said. "The little tyke didn't make it. Sorry, ma'am." Marylou ran screaming and sobbing into her bedroom still clutching her baby and climbed into her bed and pulled the covers over them. Her baby had died. How could it be? Something in Marylou also died.

When she came to see me ten years later, she could not recall much of what had happened. She vaguely felt Ralph had taken Alan away and her sister had come. There were papers to sign, and there was the funeral. She was in a fog. She said, "I can't remember any of it. I wanted to die. I still do, but I plod on. I don't care anymore—not about much of anything. I work."

She called me because she had seen an interview about my work around birth traumas. She thought she might be able to talk to me about the death of her baby. She told me that some nights she would wake up screaming and crying, and it concerned her. Maybe she needed some help. We agreed to meet weekly or more often if she wanted to.

In the decade since the death of baby Alan, she had ended her relationship with Ralph, become a successful lawyer, and moved into a high-rise condo downtown near her office. It was convenient. Often she worked late. She had tried online dating a few times and hated it. She was no longer interested in any kind of a romantic relationship. Her mother had passed away, but she and her sister were close. When she spoke of her baby, she spoke in a monotone and never used the baby's name. She showed no emotion, as if she were coldly litigating a case in court. When the session was over, she would say "Thank you" and leave the office. This was the pattern for several weeks.

The pain of the death of her baby had left a deadlock on her feelings, certainly of talking about the baby or even mentioning his name. She had gone back to work as soon as possible and had called the Salvation Army to come and pick up everything in what had been the nursery. Whenever the door to that repressed trauma cracked open a little, she would quickly change the subject.

One day the door opened, and there was a flood of tears. Her words were drowned in the flood. She could not stop. Fortunately, she was my last client for the day, and I simply stayed present with her, witnessing her grief and pain. She reached out for my hand and fell into my arms. I held her there for a long time as she sobbed. My jeans were wet from her tears. Her carefully coifed hair was a wet tangle, and her tailored lawyer's suit was rumpled and damp. Slowly, she began to talk about baby Alan. Her speech was halting and punctuated with sobs, but I knew the dam had broken and that there would be healing of some kind in the future.

In the months ahead, she shared her story with me in bits and pieces—how much she had wanted to have a baby of her own, to hold him, and watch him grow up into a fine young man. She shared her hopes and dreams for him. Session after session, hour after hour, the complete story was revealed: the early contractions, the embarrassment, the rush to the hospital, the fear she felt of the C-section, and the joy of bringing baby Alan home. The tears were sprinkled throughout the telling.

One day she spontaneously began talking to her baby. So much love spilled out from her heart. My eyes were also wet. Later, she talked about her life since baby Alan had died. She had become rigid and controlling, which was helpful to her as a lawyer. She was always in control of what she said and did—even how she dressed and walked. There was no room for feelings or spontaneity. No joy. She lived her life as a performance, and she never mentioned baby Alan. Never! She did well in her performance. It was safer that way, but she was not really alive. She began to question her life and look at opportunities to explore. She moved out of the condo near her office and bought a small house on the edge of the city. It had a large back yard and a cozy room with a fireplace she could use as a home office.

On her ride home from the city, she daily passed an animal shelter and could hear the barking and crying of the dogs. One day she stopped, parked her car, and went in. She was curious to see if the dogs and cats (she assumed both) were properly cared for. They were, and she was impressed. She walked along the cages and looked at the "incarcerated" animals. In one of the last cages, she saw one puppy who was curled up in a corner. She stopped, and the puppy got up and slowly walked toward her and sadly whimpered to her. That was it! She adopted her. She made the arrangements and was given a blanket and complimentary bag of kibble. On the way out, she saw a large older dog, a beautiful retriever. She paused and said a few kind words. The retriever slowly got up and came over to her. She knelt down and put her hand through the wire fencing and received a big wet tongue on her hand. But one dog was enough.

That night, the puppy cried a lot. The following day, Marylou returned to the dog shelter and adopted the Golden Retriever so the puppy, now named Bella, would have company during the long days she was at work.

In caring for the two dogs, Marylou began to enjoy the enthusiastic welcome they gave her when she came home from work. They followed her around and sat at her feet when she was working or reading. The little puppy would curl up beside the retriever. She began to sit with them and cuddle the puppy in her arms and relax! She had rescued them from possible death. Now they were rescuing her from a long, dark time in her life. She started to tell me about her canine companions and how sweet and loveable they were. She began looking at her life in a different way. Now there were possibilities, some classes she wanted to attend, and places she wanted to visit. She had opened her home to two sad, abandoned dogs. In turn, they led her out of a long, dark tunnel of grief. Alan would always be in her heart. She would occasionally feel his absence in her life, but she no longer lived her life in a shroud of constant grief, shut down from living life fully and from feeling joy. She now had the possibility of love in her life.

Summing Up

Often there is no opportunity for parents to hold and talk to an infant who has died, since the body of the baby is immediately taken away and disposed of. Time and compassionate respect are needed for the parents, especially the mother, to grieve and find some kind of closure.

Rachel's unusual experience of contact with a brother who had died decades before happened when she was in an open, peaceful, altered state of consciousness. Perhaps as a baby, she had had access to her mother's history and the contents of her mother's repressed consciousness. What we do know is that Rachel was successful in bringing the memory of her brother back into the family. The shadow of Jonathan David was lifted, even if long after his birth and perhaps only for a fleeting moment.

Her mother continued to refuse to talk about Jonathan David with her second son, but Rachel recognized, accepted, and experienced his brief life and made him real. He was now a part of the family's history.

Jonathan David's sense of not being seen or acknowledged mirrored Rachel's feelings within the family. By commemorating his birth and death with a private ceremony and the planting of a special bush at his gravesite, Rachel was able to honor and witness his memory and honor herself. For Rachel, Jonathan David's message was a gift in multiple ways, some of which she had not anticipated. She found a long sought-after connection with her mother and validation of her emotional sensitivity that previously had been minimized by other family members.

Karen similarly treated her experience of loss in a healing way. Whatever the age of a fetus when death occurs, it should be treated in the way that Karen did.

Unfortunately, when there is a terrible loss in a life, it is common to shut it away. The loss is so painful that no one wants to talk about it. However, traumas not processed—cried about, talked about—lie in the unconscious mind and gain traction through time. Healing comes by talking about the trauma and expressing the feelings. Only then can freedom form the past come, and with it the ability to love again.

8

Twin Spirits:

Enmeshment and the Loss of a Twin

Since Humankind's earliest days, explanations have been sought for the phenomenon of twins. Religious beliefs, cults, rituals and superstitions have been developed around these "instant siblings" in almost every culture. Myths and legends about twins emphasize aspects, often bizarre and mystical, that set them apart from the general population. Whether the occurrence of twins is considered inspiring or threatening, twins and other multiple births always aroused curiosity.

ELIZABETH NOBLE, *Having Twins* (1)

Womb life is not identical for twins, their position counts.

ARTHUR JANOV, *Life Before Birth (65)*

The loss of a child at any age is considered one of life's most painful tragedies. But the death of an infant at birth, after months of care and anticipation, causes a unique anguish that is shared by everyone involved. The loss of a twin at birth is a compounding of that grief. During the pregnancy, the parents have been seeing the two babies in their mind's eye and planning for the two infants as constant companions for one another, sharing identical or similar physical and emotional characteristics, as if destined to be the best of friends.

The bittersweet loss of one twin and the survival of the other creates an experience of pain and joy, indeed of loss and fulfillment, all in the same breath. Beset by heartache and anguish, the parents and extended family struggle to go through the stages of grief and, simultaneously, to access the support systems of family, friends, and professionals in order to be present and loving for the twin who has survived.

Equally important to consider is the loss experienced by the surviving twin. The generally accepted belief that infants do not feel pain and will not remember has been thoroughly disproved by research and clinical data. Even before birth, biology dictates the fetus is sentient, responsive, and adapting to his environment. If one twin dies at birth, the other surely knows and feels the loss.

Blighted Twin Syndrome

The prenatal loss of a twin is frequently referred to as the blighted or vanishing twin syndrome. When the early sonogram shows two babies, the doctor announces, "Twins!" At the next appointment, there is only one heartbeat—the second fetus has vanished or been absorbed or sloughed off in a small show of blood. The remaining twin's body and brain holds the memory, which may appear later in confusing or misunderstood reactions.

This syndrome is now known to be quite common. In the *Journal of Prenatal & Perinatal Psychology & Health,* Althea Hayton (2010) wrote that "a comprehensive study of twin and multiple pregnancies carried out in the early 1990s in the United States came to the astonishing conclusion that for every pair of twins who make it to birth alive, there are ten womb survivors born alone whose twin has died at some point during the pregnancies" (p.35). These early losses may not even be detected by the outside world, yet may be felt by the surviving twin.

Unfortunately, too often the mother is not allowed to grieve. Sometimes the medical professionals involved do not mention the loss, but the mother may feel something has gone wrong. In a conspiracy of silence, her feelings are not acknowledged.

Later loss is clearly more dangerous and difficult for the mother, both emotionally and physically. But without a doubt, the loss of a twin sibling in the womb is also a part of the surviving twin's experience. After all, the two have shared an environment as intimate as any two human beings can have. They grew together, moved in relationship to one another, heard the same sounds, and adapted to a world that was plural, not singular.

With ultrasound technology, we can now see into the world of the womb. Twins have been seen fighting, touching, and even kissing. They are definitely in a relationship and aware of one another or of others sharing their space. Naturally, if one twin leaves, the surviving twin senses that loss.

Years ago, when I heard a colleague talking about the blighted twin syndrome, I must say I was dubious. By the time I read scientific research proving it, I had accumulated ample evidence from experiences of my clients in pre- and perinatal therapy, and I firmly believed in the syndrome. Almost without exception, my clients had no previous knowledge of having a twin and were stunned by the discovery. With the knowledge came some sense of relief, as things in their lives began to make more sense. The long, gnawing emptiness they felt was no longer a mystery.

Sarah

A client of mine named Sarah came to therapy quite depressed and desperate. Her third marriage was on the verge of collapse. She reported a long history of feeling abandoned. Her inner world of chatter was relentlessly critical and judgmental. She said harshly, "I never let myself off the hook." She also felt guilt-ridden and as if she did not deserve anything "good" in life and needed to be punished. These mostly unconscious beliefs sabotaged her life and chance of happiness. Although she was intelligent and attractive, her life was littered with losses and broken relationships.

One day while she was in treatment, she slipped into a deep uterine memory. Words poured out of her: "There's supposed to be two . . . now there's one . . . I'm all by myself . . . You were supposed to be with me." In tears, Sarah mumbled, "You left me. I need to make a choice, go forward or back." Then, "I left him. I let go of his hand."

By this time, she was crying hard and shouting, "Oh my God, I didn't mean to . . . Oh my God, I am so sorry. I let go. He's all gone." Sobs racked her body, now rolled into a tight fetal position, as if she were holding on for her life. She paused to catch her breath only to continue to yell and cry. As her sobs began to ebb, she whispered, "Bad, bad, bad. I'm bad, bad, bad."

Gradually, Sarah calmed down and grew quiet. She now had new insights and connections that were making sense to her and offered her some clarity. The definitive meaning she had given to the event of being "bad, bad, bad" had poisoned her life and her relationships. The most deadly effect was on her relationship with herself. Entrenched in a cloak of guilt, she had made decisions and taken actions that reinforced her self-imposed sentence.

With her release of long-held emotions and her newfound awareness, she began to forgive herself and let go of the mantle of guilt and self-reproach. As she continued in therapy, that mantle slipped from her narrow shoulders, and she was able to stop punishing herself. She was finally free to explore her life with self-respect and openness to "the good things."

Greg

Another client named Greg had an experience of loss similar to Sarah's experience. Greg was a depressed, educated, middle-aged man who came to one of my residential group sessions. He had a history of alcoholism and unsuccessful relationships. He had been sober for several years.

When he talked about his depression, he talked about loss. He said, "I have always felt sad, as if I am missing someone. I have serial relationships in which I am always looking for that mysterious someone."

In spite of being withdrawn and somewhat uptight, Greg began to relax and talked openly with me. After a series of meetings, I asked him if he wanted to explore details of his birth experience. He was skeptical but willing. His knowledge during his intake interview had been scanty; however, he believed his birth had been normal without any unusual occurrences.

During one of our sessions, there was a long period of stillness and silence. I shifted my position and accidentally touched him, but lightly. He then seemed to shoot up off the mat as if he had been given a jolt of electricity. I was startled. Next, without saying anything, he inexplicably began to cry deep, heartbreaking sobs. I sat very still in order not to interfere with his emotional flood. He began to utter words about "losing him." Phrases tumbled out as he cried. "I am so sorry. Why did you leave me? Why did you go?"

I wondered who the object of his questioning and longing was. I assumed it was his mother. I was wrong. As Greg began to return to present-time awareness, he slowly opened his eyes, looked at me, and finally said, "I had a twin brother." Then he began to cry again.

I sat quietly beside him. In over thirty years of doing this profound and deep exploration with people, I have learned to not interfere or interrupt when clients are in a deep, altered state of consciousness. My therapeutic skills are available if needed, and I remain as an honored witness to the wisdom of the psyche. During an emotional release like Greg's, it is common for words or lyrics to come that seem unfamiliar or disconnected from what the individual has always believed. The surprise is often voiced as "Where did that come from?"

Greg's body relaxed, and his voice became soft and tender, as if he were speaking from a deep place of knowing. His words were now more to himself than to me. He felt a twin brother had miscarried at some point during their mother's pregnancy. In fact, he sensed he had always known about this in some place buried within his mind—from the deep recesses of his consciousness came an insight or a knowing. Greg didn't have empirical facts to prove what he had uncovered, but he knew it to be true, and he felt an intense pain of loss and grief. When some time had passed, he started to feel the presence of his brother's spirit.

Later, he shared with me his belief that he had been unconsciously searching for his twin brother all his life—in all of his relationships. After learning about the loss of his twin, he was able to sense his brother's existence in his life. In retrospect, he felt his brother had always been with him.

Now he was able to consciously grieve his loss, and his chronic depression gradually lightened. He had a new appreciation for and acceptance of himself. At last, he had closure, and with it came peace.

Clara and Claudia

The story of Clara and Claudia is not one of guilt or loss but rather of an intriguing enmeshment, woven with strong fibers of a shared history, far-reaching geography, and love. Initially, I became acquainted with Clara when she worked as a secretary in the surgery department of a prestigious medical school on the West Coast. She had read about my work in the university newspaper and decided to see me professionally to find some resolution to a deepening depression.

We met for several months in my office and explored causes and solutions to her problems. Her deep compassion for family and friends, as well as for animals and nature, was very clear. Equally clear was the strength of loyalty and sense of responsibility she felt both professionally and personally. These qualities were especially strong in the relationship she had with her twin, Claudia. Their lives had taken them to different places with different experiences; however, the connection between them never dimmed or wavered. At the time we started our work, they were living together in a small house not far from the university and a Catholic retreat center, where they sometimes volunteered and attended Mass.

One day, Clara told me the story of her birth. She was born on a cold December night in a hogan in northern Arizona where her parents had sought shelter. Although hogans—circular structures made of logs, lumber, and mud—are traditionally associated with the Navajo, this winter night's abode with blankets hanging against the walls for added protection seemed to her parents to be just the right place to give birth to their Chiricahua Apache baby. Clara was born into this welcoming world only to be handed off with a sense of urgency as another identical baby girl was about to be born. Quickly, her parents placed the twin sisters who so perfectly mirrored one another in the same wool blanket.

The young parents with French, German, and Native American roots had each been abandoned as babies and then brought up by Anglos who had taken them under their wings and also educated them. The new parents were beginning a family of their own in a traditional Native American home. In this most magic of moments, they called upon the wisdom of their rich cultural heritage and simply made a bed for their new daughters using a cardboard box with a light bulb hanging overhead for additional warmth.

Much like their nomadic ancestors, the twin girls were often on the move. They grew up in states that stretched from Connecticut to California. But when the girls were only thirteen years old, their parents divorced. The girls moved with their mother from Chicago to a multiethnic neighborhood in New York City. Their mother was an interior designer who Clara described as always beautifully dressed and very glamorous. Next, they moved to Connecticut, again finding a community with a full international flavor. Soon, their mother remarried, and they moved yet another time, now to New Jersey, which their mother thought was the safer place for her twins. They lived there for several years in a diverse, friendly neighborhood and attended a nearby

Catholic school. Later, they returned to Chicago, where Clara had a short-lived marriage.

In their early twenties, after years of being on the move, the twins decided to live together again. Both women were creative and skillful, and they helped each other navigate the challenges facing young women in the 1960s. Their homes were always nicely adorned with artifacts that clearly represented their strong Native American beliefs as well as their allegiance to Catholicism.

Clara believed Claudia was the strong independent one and watched as she saw her twin marry an actor and, following his departure to Europe, give birth to their baby boy. That marriage ended, and later Claudia had a second son with another man. As the years proceeded, Clara evolved into the strong, responsible one, whereas Claudia was sickly and often depressed. Their former roles seemingly reversed when Clara became their main financial support, although she reported feeling that "Claudia always held us together in spite of all her problems."

It was about this time that Clara learned I was making a videotaped film on regression therapy, and it piqued her interest. She volunteered to be taped if I would take her back to the time of her birth. I agreed to her request and reassured her we would stop the tape at any time. We set a date.

Much to my surprise, Clara appeared accompanied by her twin sister, Claudia. As if fitting her original template, Claudia was again the unexpected arrival! I asked Clara why Claudia had come along, and with the hint of a mischievous glint in her eyes, Clara responded, "Well, she was with me then, so why not now?" I don't think any of us had high expectations for the session. For Clara and Claudia, it was more of a curiosity, if not an adventure, and for me, it was about learning to videotape a work session.

We arranged the room with mats and pillows so each person would be comfortable and set up the camera, which was quickly forgotten. Everyone settled in and began a process of breathing deeply and relaxing. The twins were resting side by side and breathing almost in unison. As they drifted back in time, I softly suggested they imagine being in a warm, watery world inside their mother's body. I remained silent, as they curled up with the hum of their even breathing and regressed to a deep state of inner-world consciousness.

Then Clara seemed to be uncomfortable and began to struggle, squirm, and wriggle away from her twin. She appeared stressed and anxious. Suddenly, Claudia grabbed Clara's foot and cried out in pitiful whimpers, "No, don't leave me," saying this over and over again as her hand tightened on Clara's foot.

Next, Clara forcefully struggled and gasped for gulps of air. Her body lurched forward and finally broke free from her sister's grip on her foot. Her sighs heaved with relief as she reached out for someone to touch and comfort her. Claudia, now left alone on the mat, was instantly terrified. She began to shake and cry. In almost her next large breath, Claudia lunged forward, presumably out of her mother's birth canal. The room felt electric. Claudia was reaching for Clara. Both twins were quivering and whimpering, much as wet puppies do in a cold, scary place. Yet they found and hugged each other and began to relax, knowing they were together again.

The regression event revealed the imprinted pattern of the lives of Clara and Claudia. The reader may be hard pressed not to recall how Jacob held onto Esau's heel in the biblical tale of Isaac and Rebekah's twin sons. Fortunately, the sisters' initial struggle did not continue into their lives as the brothers' battle for Isaac's blessing, along with its inherent power, continued in theirs. Instead of being a story of rivalry and conflict, theirs is a story in which twins complement one another and naturally create unity. This harmony occurred with Clara and Claudia, even as they lived amidst many cultures as Native people in America. They were able to retain their core beliefs and way of being in the world in the midst of an uncertain, contemporary society.

Indeed, the pattern for the twin sisters remained the same, with Clara being the responsible, hardworking caretaker, clearly engaged in the outer world, while Claudia stayed close to home and struggled with illness, drugs, relationships, and children. For most of their lives, they not only lived together, but also saw each other through loss and gain as well as relationship struggles. The two kind-hearted women shared their love for animals and honored both their Christian and Native American traditions. Their mutual love for order and beauty was evident in all of their dwellings.

Sadly, Claudia died in 2011. Fortunately, her sons and her sister were with her in her last moments, but the time since has been a very difficult time for Clara because she so painfully misses Claudia's company in every aspect of her life.

Perhaps there is no closer relationship than that of identical twins who have been connected since conception. The two women shared their mother's womb, their births, their lives, a love for each other, and a love for Claudia's children and grandchildren. They were connected by love and a lifetime friendship. They were twins in every sense of the word.

Summing Up

Research has determined that up to 70 percent of all twins conceived are unable to make it to full term. There are now books, websites, and international organizations such as Twinless Twins to help those who live with a persisting emptiness as they face the challenge of being left behind as the surviving twin. Even though there may not be any conscious knowledge that there has been a twin, what remains is a shadowy unease. The emotions and persisting effects of these prenatal traumas affect the surviving twin and surface in therapy. Often, the unresolved traumas last indefinitely in haunting ways—in attitudes, behaviors, and dysfunctional relationships—until they are resolved in therapy or in seemingly miraculous transformational events.

The loss of her twin was painful and distressful to Sarah and cast a long shadow over years of her life. Unfortunately, traditional psychology does not explore the important, very early developmental time when the brain of the fetus is growing and responding to the environment being provided by the mother, so the prenatal causes of a client's distress or pain are rarely uncovered.

Although there are a number of accounts of twins in a conflicted or adversarial relationship almost from the start, the cultural archetype of twins is clearly one of true connection, for better or for worse.

After Clara read this chapter, she sent this response:

It [the chapter] is wonderful and brings back so many memories as I celebrate Claudia's third year of going to heaven (May 4, 2011.) She let go of my hand with a warm final touch. I will feel it every day for the rest of my life. Maybe one day I will let her go . . . I often think . . . I was first to come into this world, and then Claudia was the first to leave me. I wonder if she made a deal with God. I often ask Him. We have great conversations—crazy as this may seem. I am finally closer to Him, now that He has Claudia.

Clara recently told me she continues to feel her beloved sister's presence in her daily life.

9

Childbearing Decisions: Challenges and Consequences

Human beings are perhaps never more frightening than when they are convinced beyond doubt that they are right.

LAURENS VAN DER POST,
The Lost World of the Kalahari

In our contemporary times, abortion has become a polarizing political issue, one characterized by strong positions and opposing beliefs that have far too often resulted in attacks on clinics and the murder of medical providers. As a therapist, I take a nonjudgmental and compassionate position. My intention is to give support and guidance as clients search their hearts and minds to discover *their* truths. My task in counseling is to help each woman make her own decision about abortion based on the truth in her heart. No matter what choice my clients make, I have been deeply moved by the depth of their willingness and courage to confront this personal and often very difficult decision.

As with all challenges brought to therapy, when a woman faces a childbearing decision, there are often other issues lurking beneath the presenting problem. For that reason, when a woman facing a childbearing decision comes to me, I take a pre- and perinatal history and a family history. I inquire about previous pregnancies, miscarriages, and, of course, the birth of my client. This is important, since her own birth may have created patterns of fear, and these patterns need to be processed. For example, pre- and perinatal trauma can cause an irrational, unconscious fear of pregnancy and childbirth that disrupts a woman's naturally positive responses. Upon discovering pregnancy, panic may erupt, causing a woman to act against her deepest desires. In therapy, she needs to uncover repressed images and memories and release old pain. She can then make clear decisions based on present-time reality, free of fear or guilt.

The client's family history also needs to be explored, since trauma can spread between branches of a family or be passed down from one generation to the next. For example, trauma in one branch of a family when a newborn dies or the mother has a miscarriage can influence decisions about pregnancy in another branch of the family. A previous abortion can influence the way the mother behaves the next time she is pregnant, and the earlier abortion can influence the way she feels about her next child. It is best to process these ghosts from the past so that the possibility of a harmful influence is erased or at least diminished.

Dr. Myriam Szejer (Szejer, 2001), a French child psychiatrist and psychoanalyst, president of a French association called La Cause des Bébés and author of *Talking to Babies, Psychoanalysis on a Maternity Ward*, has found that telling suffering newborn babies their family history has astonishing therapeutic effects. At the request of doctors, she is invited into maternity wards to work with the babies facing life and death crises. Applying her philosophy of communication, she tells the baby its family history. As amazing as it seems, the baby's suffering disappears.

In early April 2001, I made arrangements to go to Paris to meet with Dr. Szeyer and talk with her about her extraordinary healing work. She told me, "I think the baby's unconscious is already present in the pregnancy and is caught up in the whole history of the family story."[1] Her work validates the amazing awareness and consciousness of infants—it is as if they are capable of being first-class psychics. The reality of her findings have been confirmed by many of the sessions of my clients. The infant seems to be present not only in the physical body of the mother but also in her mental body. This finding highlights the importance of being careful about what we say to babies and how we say it.

If patterns are not processed, they may be repeated, as was the case with one of my clients who insisted that she had no feelings at all about her four abortions. Through guided imagery, I took her back to the first time she learned she was pregnant. She had been overjoyed! However, there wasn't anyone to support her in having the child. She denied her happiness and proceeded to have her first abortion, cutting herself off from any feelings. Her subsequent abortions were a repeat of the first one—mechanical, almost robot-like, and without any emotion. In therapy, she finally felt the grief and loss of the baby she had really wanted. After further therapeutic work, she expressed a new desire to have a child, a buried wish that she finally fully acknowledged and fulfilled.

When women are not given the choice of safe abortion, they often resort to "back alleys" and do-it-yourself methods, which put them in highly vulnerable positions. They are forced to lie about the experience and with no support, feeling guilty, angry, and judged, they are robbed of the opportunity for counseling and healing. Fortunately, it is never too late to begin to heal these wounds.

What is not well known or accepted is the effect on the infant when the abortion fails. Many of the survivors of failed abortions have a death wish. Even some of the most "healed" feel they are swimming upstream, fighting some gnawing belief that they should not be present.

One of my clients made this statement:

I have always wondered why I have difficulties accepting love and praise. Over the years and endless hours of psychotherapy, I have learned that I was conditioned to prove my right to life by doing things, rather than being. Twice my mother tried to abort me, unsuccessfully, but imprinting my psyche that I was not destined to live. I was not supposed to "be."

All my life I have been driven to prove my worth and myself. Since I do not know how to be, or who to be, I have focused all my attention on what I do, primarily my work. It is no surprise to me that I became a workaholic, working sixteen to eighteen hours a day until my body could no longer stay awake. If I did not keep up with this stringent regimen, I suffered from debilitating migraines. My obsessive work habits have been dealt with in therapy, but to this day, I find it hard to be me without doing something. I also have never been free of the notion that I was not meant to live on this earth. I am alive by default.

These early imprints are difficult to change. It takes time and perseverance to end years of habituated beliefs and attitudes around which our defenses and personas have been built. Learning to validate and forgive ourselves so we can accept the love given to us is a gradual process. We must learn to be our true Self, nurturing and welcoming the child within.

Sylvia

Sylvia was in her seventies when she came to see me. She had a long history of alcoholism and had been in recovery for several years. In the process of therapy, she told me about an abortion she had when she was a young woman. She was in love with a man who was totally unacceptable to her family. Her father, a prominent physician, threatened to kill the man if he caught them together. When she became pregnant, she was terrified. She found a doctor who agreed to perform the abortion, which was illegal at the time. In his office with other patients waiting outside the door, he terminated the pregnancy. He admonished her not to make a sound and never to tell anyone. He gave her no anesthesia for the pain. Ashamed, humiliated, alone, terrified, and in pain, she did as she was told. After the procedure, trying to appear normal, she left the office and walked down the busy street. She passed by a bar, abruptly went inside, and had the first drink of her life. It dulled her pain, and from that moment, drinking became her way of surviving. She never spoke of her abortion.

Plagued by the guilt and shame, Sylvia punished herself. How different life might have been for her if she had been able to freely choose with loving support from her family and society. Instead, she later married an alcoholic and never had any children. It would be years later that Sylvia and her husband both came to STAR, where she found resolution and peace from the trauma of her abortion.

Joan

Joan came into my office in an agitated state after discovering she was pregnant from a casual affair. Marriage was out of the question, and she was clear that she wanted to terminate the pregnancy. She became calmer as we talked, and she considered a number of options. None of them felt right to her. I asked Joan to lie down and breathe deeply for a few minutes. She sank into a relaxed and peaceful state. Then I asked her to invite the spirit of the child to be with us. I requested that she explain in detail all her feelings and thoughts about being pregnant and that she dialogue with the consciousness of the child.

Two days later, Joan called to say she had a spontaneous miscarriage. She believed that the infant's soul had chosen to leave, perhaps to come again at a later time. As it would happen, Joan did become pregnant again a few years later, and this time quite happily so—she felt the circle had been made whole again.

Travis

Travis was affected by his grandmother's early attempt to abort his mother. He shared this story with me.

My mother told me about the time when she was about six to seven months pregnant with me and happened to overhear a conversation between her mother and aunt. Mom was walking down the hallway in her parents' home, and upon hearing her name mentioned in hushed tones, she stopped to eavesdrop. Visiting in the kitchen nook were my grandmother and great aunt. Mom leaned against the wall and listened. Her mother was talking about the time she tried to abort her, my mother! Mom said she "almost fell to the floor." When the subject changed between the two, Mom sneaked back to her room, me in her belly. Soon after this event, Mom was back in Atlanta, alone with my dad. At nine months pregnant, she stumbled and fell down a flight of stairs—yet another shock to her and to me. I wouldn't come for another three weeks. Goodness knows why I didn't want to come out!

I remember my birth vividly, too. The feelings of poison, the color green, a sickly green, sickly green milk . . . then the bright lights and the pain.

I have always been lactose intolerant and have had severe problems like my mother, her brother, and my grandmother. I wonder if there is any connection?

Could Travis as a prenate have been afraid to come out or be born? We now know that prenates sense their mother's emotions. The shock that Travis's mother felt surely resonated in her womb, as did the harsh impact of her fall down the stairs. As Travis's experience shows, we are more connected than we realize to the experiences of those who came before us.

Elsa

At the recommendation of her therapist, Elsa came to stay at our ranch therapy center in northern California. She had been born unwanted in Berlin after the end of World War II. Her family was very poor, and they struggled in the post-war era. Her siblings were older, having been born before the war. When her father returned from the battlefield, he was missing an arm. He became a severe alcoholic. The last thing Elsa's mother wanted was another child. Many years later, her mother told Elsa that she attempted to abort Elsa several times. Each attempt had failed, and Elsa had been born—afraid and unwanted.

Elsa's mother and father were both physically and emotionally abusive to her. They didn't bother to name her for months. To make matters worse, later, her older brother sexually abused her—with her father's knowledge! Elsa learned to escape by disassociating, but the continuing neglect and abuse eventually led to crisis intervention by authorities. She was sent to a state school, where she was provided meals and medical attention. No one ever spoke of the psychological damage being done to this little girl, but they did notice that she was starving to death and fed her. It was years later that Elsa confronted the abuse of her childhood.

When her embittered father committed suicide, he left a note blaming everything on Elsa. This message, like all the messages she received from her abuse, worked to invalidate her right to exist and filled her with guilt for being alive. Tellingly, Elsa's earliest memories were of playing in the rubble that remained following the bombings in Berlin.

When Elsa grew older, she left her family and came to New York, where she acquired a job as a nanny. She worked her way through undergraduate and graduate school, earning a PhD in psychology. She became a counselor in a private school and was beloved by her students for her compassionate understanding.

However, the strain of her early traumas often continued to torment her. The weight of it simply felt too great, and she would find herself in a disassociated state, huddled in a corner like a wounded animal and unable to speak English (her native tongue was German.) She learned how to recognize early signals of these disassociated states and would find a safe place until they passed and she could once again "behave." She had rare times of freedom and ease.

Elsa's therapy was long and arduous, yet she made progress in transforming her original traumatic imprint. While at the ranch, my Chocolate Labrador, Dulce, started following Elsa around. Soon they became inseparable, and she reported to me that being with Dulce was the first time she felt truly loved. One day I asked her if she would like

Dulce to sleep in her cabin. In a state of disbelief, she asked if that would be possible. I told her I was the boss, and I said yes. When Dulce became pregnant, it was Elsa who helped deliver the nine puppies. Before Elsa left the Ranch, I gave her one puppy from that litter, which she took home with her.

One day she told me that every time she saw an accident on the highway, her first instinctive thought was "Oh, good! Maybe someone will die." I will never forget her words. The imprint from the womb remained deep in her consciousness. The first message of her life was "You should not be here."

Elsa's story is a stark illustration of the power of primal imprints. Those words came directly from the deepest imprint in her life. Her vital reference point for creating a meaningful life was her empathy for her students. She consistently gave to others what she had needed: understanding, kindness, generosity, and love.

Summing Up

For many women, the decision to have an abortion is an easy one. For others, it is an agonizing decision. In either scenario, there are consequences to be considered. Like so many traumas and crises, abortion is an issue that can linger after the initial difficult decision has been made. It can be reflected later in a woman's future pregnancies and have an impact on succeeding generations, as Travis's story shows. It can be seen as a blessing or a curse, a relief or a lifelong burden of shame and guilt.

Each woman, in considering these difficult and personal issues, deserves counseling as well as access to all available information about support groups, social agencies, and financial assistance. Armed with this data, she is better equipped to find the help she needs to make her decision wisely. With patience and knowledge, women and men can arrive at their best decision without guilt or shame.

It is wise for women who have had miscarriages, stillborn babies, or natal losses of any kind to seek counseling before they become pregnant again or adopt a child. The original wound needs to be healed. If feelings are repressed, old fears may cloud future pregnancies and relationships.

Adults who as children were strongly unwanted or even hated often feel as if they are "bad," and they want to be punished or to punish others, including their own children. They will find many ways to use punishment on themselves or others, including by projecting their "badness" onto their own children and punishing them to make them "good." When there is an unconscious message of this kind, there is often an unwillingness to be fully present. They may not seek a physical death, but they may live shadowy lives that make them feel safe. They may close their hearts to accepting themselves and to receiving the support and acceptance they crave and deserve.

Fortunately, children with psychosis because of very early, often life-threatening trauma can be helped with therapy that allows them to revisit the original trauma, release it, and learn to love the child they once were. This process has the potential to end their constant need to prove to themselves that they deserve to live. They learn to stop projecting their badness and forgive themselves and open their hearts to give and receive the love they deserve.

However, with continued abuse and neglect, children may become part of the explosion of violence in our communities, particularly the explosion of violence among children and teens. Violence in the womb and infancy breeds violence. Ghosts from the nursery will seek revenge.

If we realize that early trauma has a cost, we can fend off harm to self or others. It is also important to know that it is never too late to begin to heal the wounds left behind by early pre- or perinatal trauma.

The most powerful time to teach love and instill a sense of self-worth is at the beginning. Love is a powerful healing energy and can triumph over fear. Even the love Elsa felt for my dog opened her heart to the experience of healing.

When we realize that much early trauma can be avoided by the way we bring our youngest members into the world, we can focus our energy on simple, natural, loving behavior and safe human connections.

10

No Safe Harbor:
The Legacy of Child Abuse

In order to understand the tier of violent behavior in which America is now submerged, we must look before pre-adolescence, before grade school, before preschool to the cradle of human formation in the first thirty-three months of life including prenatal development.

ROBIN KARR-MORSE and MEREDITH S. WILEY,
Ghosts from the Nursery: Tracing the Roots of Violence

While an ethic of justice proceeds from an ethic of equality—that everyone should be treated the same—an ethic of care rests on the premise of nonviolence—that no one should be hurt.

CAROL GILLIGAN, *In a Different Voice*

You might think that little babies would escape the physical and emotional torment of the world, but they do not. On October 18, 2015, Christopher Ingraham, a guest of Alex Witt's *Weekend Show* on MSNBC (2015), reported that every week of that year, there had been an accidental shooting by a toddler with access to a gun. Although he went into more exacting detail, the main point was that the numbers added up to forty-three shootings that year by innocent infants! Many children needlessly die in war-torn countries, insurgencies, or refugee camps, which is hard enough to make sense of, but this news of toddlers and guns in the United States is shocking and a disgrace.

Apart from the challenges the United States faces because of the easy accessibility of guns, alarming statics highlight the challenges the United States faces with incidents of child abuse. How is it that the United States, an industrialized, technologically sophisticated nation, ranks so poorly (fifth) in the world in terms of child abuse? The Childhelp website at wwww.childhelp.org has indicated that 80 percent of the twenty-one-year-olds who reported being abused as children met the criteria for having at least one psychological disorder. Individuals who reported six or more adverse childhood experiences had an average life expectancy that was two decades shorter than those who reported none.

Many explanations account for what might drive an adult to abuse or kill a child, including drugs, poverty, mental disease, and marital conflicts. Mercifully, not all children who suffered abuse grow up to be abusers. Many receive enough nurturing by someone or some social resource, so they are spared their conflicted history and instead directed toward a path of nonviolence. Many of the survivors of abuse grow up to lead fulfilling lives, but many do not. All carry within them the unprocessed anger, grief, and pain from the abuse they suffered. Until they revisit and process their own traumas, there remains a danger that they will lose control and act out their pain on someone else. Children, at any age, are easy targets. A crying baby, a stubborn five-year-old—even something as benign as a spilled glass of milk or a messy diaper—can trigger a furious outburst of physical and emotional abuse.

Because of our anger at the perpetrator and our immediate compassion for the child, we are not able to see or are not interested in understanding the pain of the abuser who was once a small, vulnerable, and terrified victim. As Alice Miller (2002) has advised us, we need to remember that violence begets violence and that the patterns are passed on. Those who abuse were very likely abused as children.

Some severely damaged children may grow into adults who function normally. They grow up, go to school, even parent children, but they have a tentative hold on a carefully crafted reality that leaves them forever at risk of a breakdown or an explosion of repressed, uncontrolled emotions. The use of prescribed medication often prevents such dangerous occasions and is therefore helpful, but masking symptoms with drugs should not be confused with healing. In addition, the media abounds with stories of violent acts committed by people who neglected their medication or who were given the "wrong dose" or "wrong prescription."

Medications are definitely valuable and necessary to help keep people safe. More permanent solutions require a better understanding of the original cause. Painful memories and repressed emotions can be safely re-experienced and drained of emotional charges so that they will not be "acted out" on innocent people, including the self. True, such genuine healing requires time, compassion, and patience. It also requires therapists who are trained not to be afraid of feelings and who have dealt with at least some of their own unresolved early pain. Genuine healing also requires courageous clients and a safe, supportive environment.

Whenever I hear of another incident where a parent or guardian has killed a child, I shiver inside. In these moments we ask ourselves, "How could this happen?" In California, where I used to live, there was a local ordinance to place signs on dumpsters urging women to not use them for abandoning their unwanted infants. Directions were posted telling parents where the infant could be safely left, with "no questions asked." It is appalling that abandoning infants in such a way has become so commonplace that the signs are necessary. Indeed, it is so common that psychologist Charles Patrick Ewing (1997), author of *Fatal Families*, has given the phenomena a name: "disappearing disposable babies." Scores of infants are abandoned every year. Society recoils and asks, "How can a mother abuse her own baby?"

Perhaps the next two stories will shed light on that question and offer new hope.

Margot

Margot attended a Star Workshop group because she had recently lost the ability to speak. She also sought therapy because she was afraid that she might harm her children.

Her childhood had been horrendous. Her mother had given away all four of her daughters at once for no apparent reason, but she had kept her two sons. Margot, only three years old at the time, was placed with a foster family. They seemed like a perfect place to leave a young child. The father was a Baptist minister and the mother was a homemaker. Behind closed doors, however, the father was a child molester, and Margot became his victim. She learned she had to be a polite, good little girl, and under no circumstances was she ever to mention the mistreatment she regularly received from her foster father. She learned to be mute about the abuse.

She grew up pretty, sweet, and very well behaved. She married a farmer who was also a successful businessman. They had two children and lived as if everything were perfect. However, after a few years, her growing anxiety prompted Margot to enter therapy. During her therapeutic work, old, repressed, and long-forgotten painful feelings began to emerge, and she literally lost her voice. That is when her therapist recommended she come to STAR, our residential treatment program.

During one session, through tears and choking sobs, she finally began to speak. "I held him under the bath water. I had to stop him from crying. I had to stop him."

She was telling the story of how she had tried to drown her first baby to stop his cries. Margot said, "I couldn't control myself. I had to make him be good."

Margot sat with her head down, hugging her knees to her chest and rocked back and forth. There was a heavy silence in the room. I waited until she continued speaking again.

This happened several times. He struggled to breathe. I'd stop myself and pick him up and cry. Then one time, I had this sudden realization. He's just like me! He just wants to live. He's just like me. I wanted to live!

She said that she had picked him up out of the water then and held him tightly as she sobbed. That was the last time she had tried to stop his cries so that he would be good.

It was clear that a powerful flood of emotion had broken through when her baby's crying restimulated her own repressed pain. As a child, she had survived by killing her feelings, by shutting up and shutting down. To avoid her pain and cope, she had become an inauthentic, sweet, obedient, "good little girl." Now, as an adult, the key to her survival and her child's seemed to be to silence her child—and in a strange way, keep the child safe—just as she had learned to silence herself.

By blurting out this terrible truth, Margot discovered herself and found her voice again—a voice that in therapy released the rage and terror she felt at being given away by her biological mother and being abused and neglected by her foster parents. Now, in seeing her own wounds projected on her baby, she opened a door to her history and realized the impact of her own early trauma.

She recalled and expressed the feelings she had swallowed when she was a little girl. With her new awareness and release, she no longer projected herself on her baby. There was no longer a need to drown his feelings to make him good and keep him safe.

Margot began to experience compassion for the child she had been. She realized that none of the abuse she had suffered had been her fault. She was not a throw-away, worthless child. Like the first green leaves on the trees in spring, her self-esteem was emerging. She heard her own voice of strength and truth, and she felt a deep understanding and love for her two children. In STAR, with facilitators present, and with the supportive strength of the other participants, she learned how to have a genuine sense of self-worth, and as she accepted herself, she was able to love her children even more.

Sally

Several years ago, I received a call from a woman named Sally who, like Margot, was afraid she might hurt her baby. With great concern, she told me that whenever her sixteen-month-old baby cried, she would feel a strong, compulsive anger and a need to make her baby stop. She feared that one day she might snap and lose her temper. This anxious young mother was caught between her love for her baby and the danger of her uncontrollable rage. She came to see me, and when I took her history, she was surprised that I asked about her own birth. No therapist had ever inquired about it, and she was curious why I felt it might be important.

Sally had been born nearly three months early. Her beautiful mother was a model for whom getting "fat" was not permissible, so she constrained her growing belly with a very strong girdle. She was not going to allow being pregnant to interfere with her life and career, including the shape of her body.

One day on a modeling assignment, Sally's mother began to hemorrhage. Rushed to the hospital, she delivered a tiny, premature daughter who was immediately placed in an incubator. There Sally stayed for approximately nine weeks. Her mother rarely came to visit.

Unfortunately, when a baby is separated from his mother, isolated except for standard physical attention, important neurological developmental patterns form that hamper the chances for the mother to bond with the infant. The degree of damage can vary depending on many circumstances, such as the length of the treatment and the severity of the trauma. In Sally's case, in addition to not being wanted, she was born at six months, and then to compound the problem, she was left alone "in a box" for over two months—a lifetime for an infant. By the time her mother took her home, it was too late. Her mother was a stranger to her. Sally was wondering, "Who is this lady?"

In this situation, the early right brain of the baby is learning coping mechanisms to adapt, indeed, to survive. It is easier to avoid contact than to experience the painful repetition of neglect or abandonment. For this reason, Sally's relationship with her mother remained strained. She did not feel close to her. In fact, she didn't even like her. Typical of avoidant attachment behavior, there was no bonding when Sally was a baby or at any time after.

As an adult, Sally projected her pain on her child whenever her baby cried, just as Margot had. Babies cry because their overwhelming biological and emotional needs for mothering demand to be met, and crying is the infant's primary means of communication. If babies' needs are not met, they finally give up! They shut up and adapt. They may also shut down. Eventually, the system may break down, exhaustion and hopelessness set in, and the depressed infant surrenders. Babies then also give up hope that the universe is friendly, that their voices matter, that someone will be there for them, and that they are lovable. They may look like they are happy, peaceful, and loving because they have learned to pretend and perform to guarantee their safety. But they have lost their authentic selves, which remain on idle deep within. Still, they long for genuine acceptance and, ultimately, genuine reassurance that they matter.

Another response by the crying baby is one of complete resistance. These babies are oppositional and angry. Their stance toward life becomes consistently defensive and isolating, directed by a self-protective protest. Sullen belligerence punctuated by occasional outbursts is their defense. Even worse, their authenticity is lost and lies in wait to be discovered. Punishment follows, and it can be violent.

Like Margot, Sally projected her pain on her baby. She had learned long ago to be very controlled and to control others, especially emotionally. Since she had shut herself down when she was a baby, she later felt driven to shut down the cries of her child. The experience of her baby's crying triggered her unresolved pain. Since her survival depended on controlling herself and her environment, it was frightening to not be able to control a crying baby.

Fortunately, in therapy, Sally was able to return to her past and heal her own painful wounds, so she was no longer in danger of hurting her child. She was finally free to be authentic, to feel, and to love.

Summing Up

Over the years, I have had many clients who feared they might lose control and hurt someone. Many lost their tempers and hurt people, harmed animals, broke objects, or smashed cars. Very likely, they had witnessed or experienced violence as children.

They are usually at a loss to explain their behavior, which is frequently at odds with their passive demeanor and mild-mannered, polite, programmed selves. It is a shock to their friends and families when they lose control. Everyone saw Margot as a sweet, helpful young woman. She had adapted and learned her good-little-girl role very well. Most of the time, she was under control and oblivious to her repressed dynamics. No one would have believed she had such rage within that she might be driven to kill her baby.

Jill Korbin (2003), anthropology professor and associate dean at Case Western University, articulated the perceptions of many when she said that "parenting is supposed to be a quintessential part of human nature, it is supposed to be instinctive." Parenting is not just supposed to be instinctive—it is instinctive. Some damage had to have happened to destroy natural instinct. Something happened to Margot and Sally to deaden their ability to defend their children. Something happened to sever the biological and instinctive drive to love and protect their young!

We know that threads of rage and fear from an individual's hidden memories weave together, forming a dangerous weapon to be used against others, including the individual's children. Unresolved, unconscious, or repressed emotions may be triggered and drive adults to violent acts. The experience of past violence or abuse is not the only cause of violence, but it plays a significant part. Statistics show that many abused children grow up to be abusers. Unfortunately, this cause of violence is usually ignored.

We saw in Margot's story how early fear constricted her ability to love. Margot said, "I didn't know what [love] was." Loving requires the heart to be open and the individual to be real and vulnerable.

It is important during the sensitive periods of brain growth that nurturing and intimacy are present. Without them, there may be permanent brain damage, which may result in later patterns of violence, depression, and aggression (Prescott, 1975). Fortunately, one person who loves and respects the child can make a difference in the child's life. That person's caretaking does not need to be perfect, but it needs to be good enough to ensure there is some sense of security. Without even "good enough" parenting, and with ongoing neglect and abuse, there is not only the absence of love, but also the presence of terror. The "hole in my heart" so frequently referred to by individuals like Margot and Sally may become a fearful cauldron of hatred and anger, cooking up an accompanying need for revenge.

In all cases, the importance of affection, bonding, touching, holding, and love cannot be overestimated. In his article, What babies are teaching us about violence, David Chamberlain (1995) confirms the importance of bonding and links the lack of bonding to the experience of violence:

> In animal studies, the profound effects of separation in the post-partum—after birth—period have been documented. And they have a profound effect on infant bonding. Separation is both a physical and emotional experience for a baby and can begin anytime in the womb or after birth. Whenever it occurs, it is a stroke of violence.
>
> Few things can compare with the oneness between mother and baby during pregnancy. The connections are total and holistic . . . embracing mind, emotion, and sensation. In this intimate world, babies know when they are not wanted, and if rejection persists, the harm worsens and infant bonding may not be possible (p.66).

A scenario in which people deliberately attempted to destroy mother-child bonding is illustrative. In Nazi Germany, the attempt was made to produce people who could not feel another person's pain, who lacked compassion, and who would make good soldiers who obeyed authority without question. According to Nazi doctor Johanna Haarer (1934), "The healthy newborn child should be separated from the mother immediately following birth, and then placed, alone if possible, in a room for the next twenty-four hours." This policy was to thwart mother and infant bonding. The Nazis also advocated "crying rooms" where infants could cry themselves out and become hardened. There were no acceptable alternatives for the harsh treatment of Dr. Haarer's victims lest they become "little tyrants."

In contrast, a group called the White Rose Society formed during the rise and reign of Adolf Hitler openly called for a revolt against his criminal regime. The resistance group believed that babies should be held, carried, and touched, that the babies' needs should be respected. They were openhearted and affectionate with their children.

These two radically opposed systems of child rearing serve as a dramatic reminder of how important it is for children to be safe, cared for, and loved if we are to have a humane and humanitarian society. Sadly, the Nazis annihilated members of the White Rose Society along with millions of others.

In his book *Tomorrow's Baby*, Dr. Thomas Verny (2002) paraphrased Dr. Bruce Perry, a neuroscientist and internationally acclaimed expert on Interrelated Phenomena: "Until we understand and address the relationship between cultural belief systems, child rearing practices and prenatal and perinatal influences, we will be unable to prevent the violence in our midst" p.194.

My intention with this chapter has been to emphasize the importance of our past and to describe the ways in which it influences both our lives and those of our children. If we incorporate this knowledge into our practices, we will have the chance to turn around the prevailing legacy of violence and provide a safe harbor for our children from the very beginning.

11

Kinship of Abuse: Violence Passed Down through Generations

If we hope to create a non-violent world where respect and kindness replace fear and hatred, we must begin with how we treat each other at the beginning of life. For that is where our deepest patterns are set. From these roots grow fear and alienation—or love and trust.

SUZANNE ARMS

The headline of an article in my local newspaper, The Santa Cruz Sentinel, caught my eye.

MOM WHO IMPRISONED DAUGHTER IN CLOSET GETS LIFE BEHIND BARS—NEARLY DEAD GIRL 8, WEIGHED 25 POUNDS.

As horrible as the story sounds, it was not surprising to me. I have heard many stories of child abuse in which, tragically, some legal ruling returned a child to an abusive parent. Courts sometimes ignore the fact that blood is not always thicker than water - that being a biological parent should not be judged more important than the health and, in some cases, the very life of the child.

In this case, authorities found a malnourished eight-year-old shut up in a closet. According to the report, "She lay there naked, in her own feces and urine, praying someone might open the door." The little girl was close to death. Her mother said she had locked her in the closet because "she was bad and didn't mind me."

Here was yet another powerful example of someone who had been an abused child and who grew up and continued the abusive pattern with her own daughter. Like other such examples, it illustrates that we learn to parent from the way we are parented, and without a great deal of effort and consciousness, we may reflexively repeat the patterns. In this way, the sins of the mothers are visited upon their children.

The original Greek definition of the word *sin* is to "miss the mark."[4] Where had the parent's lineage in this story missed the mark? Where do we place the blame? Do we blame a war, a famine, poverty, or just one abusive ancestor?

There is a popular tendency now to blame everything on a gene. TV programs have stories about individuals with a "criminal gene" or an "addictive gene." It is so much tidier to blame genetics. People find it easier to say an abusive mother had an "abuse gene" than to untangle the webs of her life that conditioned her to behave with such cruelty toward her child.

This belief in genetic determinism is popular in spite of the latest research showing that genes change to fit the environment, which makes the environment the determining factor. This is why Dr. Bruce Lipton says, "Genetic determinism may be nothing more than belief determinism."[5] Patterns of behavior, ways of perceiving the world, and attitudes are passed on to the next generation and the next like tried and true recipes for potato salad.

Perhaps you have heard the story of the young woman who asked her mother why she always cut off the end the ham before baking it. The response was "My mother always did." The story leads back to the great-grandmother whose pan was too small to hold a whole ham, so she had to cut the ham. Holding on to the past like a threadbare security blanket blinds us to using bigger pans that are readily available instead of mindlessly cutting the ham. While we hold on to the past, we may not see current opportunities as positive changes in our lives or as a chance to grow in awareness.

The newspaper article writer discussed the childhood of the abusive mother. As is frequently true of generational stories, the characters blend together, and reports about the individuals may become confusing. The stories also take on a familiarity and reveal patterns that are repeated in various years and locations. For the sake of clarifying the generations in this story, I have elected to call the grandmother "Helen," her daughter "Lily," and Lily's eight-year-old daughter "Megan."

This is the story of the sins of one generation passing to the next. None of these babies were born into an emotionally secure environment. If there is blame, it falls on our society and its misguided systems that do not care to understand. When will we realize that a child's well-being should have the highest priority?

Helen, Lily, and Megan

For the first three years of Lily's life, Lily's mother, Helen, who was a prostitute and a drug addict, neglected her. We can only guess at Lily's prenatal stress, developmental factors, birth traumas, and lack of bonding. We can also only speculate about the ability of her drug-addicted mother to respond appropriately to her baby's needs. Certainly the biological responses required by a baby to feel loved and safe in the world must have been compromised. After struggling for three years, Helen decided to give Lily up for adoption.

As part of her lawyers' defense against child abuse, Lily testified about her traumatic childhood. She reported that she had never felt loved by her adoptive parents. This inability to trust is understandable, for after three years of neglect and abuse by her biological mother, Lily's ability to trust and be vulnerable enough to accept love may have become impossible or at best very difficult for her. This is a common symptom among children with attachment disorders. It is also a valid predictor of future problems, especially in terms of the individual's ability to relate positively to other people, including her own children.

Like Lily, many traumatized individuals live life on the defensive, and trusting others is frightening for them. As Lipton writes, "Pre-natal trauma can lock a newborn in a chronic sympathetic nervous response to life, a hyper-vigilant stance to life."[6]

Lily's primary lessons in parenting came from her first three years of life with her biological mother. Those lessons had been thoroughly imprinted before she ever saw the second mother, her adoptive mother. In all likelihood, Lily was destined to act out those patterns with her own children if she became a parent.

There wasn't any information available about Helen's childhood. It is logical to assume that Helen had been traumatized and was an earlier link in the chain of abuse. She probably learned parenting from how she was parented and passed both the lessons and the damage to the next generation. This is how trauma cascades from mother to daughter to granddaughter.

The news article did contain additional information about the defendant. Lily grew up, got pregnant, and gave birth to Megan. Then she gave Megan up for adoption, just as she had been given up for adoption. Much later, Lily said she "regretted it." She believed that her adoptive mother would love her more if she got her baby back. So Lily set out to get custody of Megan in the vain hope that she (Lily) would be loved by her adoptive mother. In most wounded psyches, there lurks the futile hope that "I will finally get what I missed" (a mother's love). This is an essential ingredient of both codependency and attachment disorders. Megan was treated as little more than a pawn.

In fact, Lily went to great lengths to get Megan away from the family who had adopted her. Due to a legal error made by the adopting parents' lawyer, she succeeded. Megan was forced to leave her family and return to live with Lily and Lily's boyfriend. She was wrenched away from the only family she had ever known. A small technicality was more important than the life and well-being of a child. To me, this does not seem like a fair exchange.

However, recovering Megan, her biological daughter, did not bring Lily the love she craved. Her twisted reasoning that her adoptive mother might love her more if she got Megan back was not the answer. Lily was seeking to fill her unmet need for maternal love, which she had never received from her biological mother and did not receive from her adoptive mother.

If we further explore this generational tale of loss and horror, we need to ask what Megan learned from all those days and nights locked in a closet because she was "bad." It might be hard for Megan to blame her mother and express the rage that must exist within her. More likely, she will grow up believing that she is a "bad girl" and deserves to be punished. If that happens, she will find partners and life situations that will be punishing for her. It won't be difficult to find them.

Very likely, neither Helen nor Lily ever experienced feeling safe and loved. The cascading effect of their pain almost caused the death of Megan, an innocent eight-year-old. What has she learned about parenting? Fortunately, she has been placed back with her adoptive family. We can only hope she is in a good situation, one where she will be fed, and her body can grow and recover. But what about her mind? Will she receive the nurturing she must have in order to mend her broken heart?

Lily, the middle female in this saga, will indeed pay her debt to society. But will there be any significant change in the system? Chances are slim because the underlying causes were not addressed. Lily was given a life sentence in prison, so perhaps society can feel vindicated. Yet what is the potential for Megan's future happiness? Megan can gain weight, and her body may grow naturally, in spite of her torture, but will her spirit ever feel free to fly? Without proper help, Megan may remain jailed within her mind, behind walls of shame, grief, fear, and anger. The memory of her despicable treatment will not fade like a photograph left too long in the sunlight. Rather, it will be repressed, laying in wait for some similar situation to emerge, and then it will be acted out. Someone will suffer. The memories of her abuse will not be easily forgotten. Repressed or not, they will remain. Without proper therapy, and consistent nurturing, chances of the vicious cycle being repeated are high. What kind of mothering love will Megan provide for her own children? Without understanding the past, we are doomed to repeat it. Only then are we free to create a different future.

Frank

Frank was a client who had been in prison for brutally attacking his ex-wife. He told me his mother had died giving birth to him. Throughout his childhood, he was shuffled from one relative to another and never spent much time with any one family. His father had abandoned him. He was neglected and isolated. He felt no one really wanted him. He was right: no one did.

During a regression in therapy, one of his first memories was of himself as a four- or five-year-old holding a hammer in his hand and screaming at a younger child, "You got yours! I want mine!" It was a shock to him to realize that he was talking about his mother. The other child had a mommy. He wanted one too! This was his unconscious hope—that someday he would be loved as a mother would have loved him.

Many years later, he married and expected his wife to fill that same empty hole in his heart. Finally, he thought, he would "have his." After several years of Frank's extreme jealousy and controlling temperament, his wife divorced him and left the state. Driven by his rage, Frank tracked her down and assaulted her, demonstrating his feeling of "If I can't have her, no one else can." All of this was certainly influenced by the lack of a significant, loving, and consistent caregiver in his early childhood. He yearned for someone to fill the emptiness he felt.

In *Ghosts from the Nursery*, Robin Karr-Morse and Meredith S. Wiley (2013) write, "The ghosts of children lost to rage and despair, overlooked or abused by a community unaware of their existence do retaliate. These children—like all children—do unto others" p.10. For Frank, the pent-up rage and unfulfilled need were expressed in his brutal assault on his wife, who was supposed to be the stand-in for the mother he never had. In Lily's story, her own little girl was the victim. When given the choice between the life of her child and the vain hope of finally getting her need for love met by her adoptive mother, there was no hesitation. For both Frank and Lily, the illusion that they could find someone to fill their bottomless well of need led to tragic consequences. Violence does not suddenly appear in full bloom. It has been growing in a culture of abuse, neglect, and pain, a culture that frequently began in the womb.

The Early Roots of Violence

Alice Miller once sent out an e-mail letter addressed to "College Students of All Nations." As in her books, she theorized that the roots of violence came from early childhood abuse or neglect. Her clarion call to students was to stem the tide of violence by stopping violence toward children. She believed, as research now verifies, that abused children are likely to grow up to become abusive and violent. In her appeal to young people, she stated, "Children are innocent at birth, and they need love, care and protection, but never violence to become compassionate adults" (Miller, 2000).

In her book *For Your Own Good* (2002), she wrote that children are not innately evil, nor do they arrive in the world as a blank slate. They have a history and are part of a larger family history. Destructive behavior, be it towards oneself or others, is a reactive pattern from the past, when the child was not protected from a painful, frightening world.

Statistics show that the highest percentage of abuse comes from the hands of the very adults charged with protecting the children—their caretakers. The Childhelp website at www.childhelp.org has revealed that reports of child abuse in the United States occur every ten seconds. This adds up to over three million reports each year involving six million children (some reports include more than one child.) The Childhelp organization has also determined that more than 70 percent of the children who died because of neglect or abuse were two years old or younger, and 80 percent of the reports involved at least one parent as the perpetrator. Described differently, children are in the greatest peril at the hands of their own caretakers. Could it be that these adult caretakers might be seeking revenge for what they suffered as children? Violence does beget violence. Yet it is crucial to note that severe neglect is equally as traumatizing.

It is well documented and accepted by most psychologists that early pain and experiences of violence are repressed in the individual's unconscious body-brain. These early experiences lay in wait to be "acted out" on others or themselves, which takes a toll not only on relationships with others, but also on the health, productivity, and well-being of the individual. This early violence can form the roots of mental illness, which can ignite further violence, other maladaptive behaviors, and addictions.

What is not recognized is that the original trauma may have occurred during the prenatal period, birth, or infancy. The disempowered and humiliated baby becomes an adult seeking to exert power over someone, or some place or time, or the disempowered and humiliated baby becomes an adult seeking punishment because that is what he learned to expect for his life.

My addition to Alice Miller's thesis would be to include the first nine months of life, for when there is danger of hostility felt in the womb, children are born already traumatized, afraid, and hypervigilant.

Tomas

One summer when I was working in Sweden, a young man made an appointment to see me. He was plagued by an unusual fear that was restricting his life. He was unable to eat anywhere other than at home without having a panic attack. He wanted to date girls, and this phobia severely limited his options, since dates usually involved some kind of restaurant setting, which he could not tolerate. His social life was at a standstill.

Tomas had always been uncomfortable in kitchens. He would eat as fast as he was able so he could be excused from the table and hurry away. His mother was aware of his kitchen anxiety but brushed it off as a childhood idiosyncrasy that he would outgrow. Going to a friend's house when food was involved or going to a restaurant was impossible for him. The anxiety had been a part of his childhood, but he was older now and wanted to deal with it. He wanted to get on with his life.

Tomas was in his early twenties when he began his therapy. I was curious about the panic attacks, and I asked Tomas to tell me about the moments when he panicked. His entire life had been restricted by the attacks, but many of the attacks he described were recent events. One day, he told me about the first overpowering attack he could clearly remember. He was nine years old, in the school cafeteria with friends at lunchtime. As usual, he was uncomfortable with the clattering of dishes and pans, but he was in control and listening to his friends.

> I was sitting at a table with some other kids, eating my lunch. The sounds of the dishes, plates, and cutlery being placed on stainless steel shelves was audible but in the background. Suddenly someone slammed a door shut. It made a very loud bang. I started screaming and ran out of the building and hid in the woods nearby. I would not go back inside. I was shaking and crying. I couldn't stop until my Mom came and rescued me.

I thought this might be a posttraumatic stress response to some earlier trauma. From that event forward, his panic attacks escalated and limited his level of tolerance. Now he would only eat at home within the safety net of his mother's kitchen. Tomas could remember nothing earlier. He was open to looking deeper into his unconscious in hopes of finding some answers.

In another therapy session, Tomas relaxed on the mat while listening to some meditation music, and with some subtle suggestions, he slipped into a deep state of peace. He was on a journey to discover the source of his panic attacks. After several sessions of recalling early childhood memories, we were unable to discover any traumatic moments. One day, I suggested to Tomas that he be very tiny in his mother's womb. Tomas curled up in a fetal position and seemed to be napping. He suddenly became agitated, and then, he began to scream, kick, and wave his hands in absolute terror. After a while, the terror and screaming subsided, and he became very quiet and still. He rested for a long time. I sat quietly. In due time, he began to talk in a subdued tone about the experience that had so horrified him.

> My mother, five months pregnant with me at the time, was standing at the kitchen sink doing dishes. My father was outside the kitchen window with a shotgun in his hand. A cat had given birth to a litter of kittens, and my father was shooting them. One last kitten remained alive, partially hidden behind the others. My father bent forward to move the kitten so he could shoot it, but he leaned onto the gun and shot himself instead. He died right there. My mother began to scream hysterically and ran out to the yard to see his bleeding, dying body slumped over on the ground.

I can only speculate how Tomas "saw" this. I can imagine the jolt of adrenaline that shot into his mother's body and into his world in the womb. We know the five-month-old fetus felt what she was experiencing—the noise of the gunshot, the terror, the panic, and the heartbreaking screams.

Tomas, now an adult, could use both right and left hemispheres of his brain to become conscious of the original trauma that lay at the source of his panic attacks. He screamed, writhed, flung his arms helplessly about, and cried. His body released a flood of emotions from the event, and his mind made sense of the reaction he experienced in the school cafeteria. Finally, he became quiet and made connections between the trauma of his father's death and his fears.

After re-experiencing the grisly episode, Tomas felt relieved and calmer. The regression allowed him to contact and release overwhelming emotions that had been poisoning his life since before he was born.

Gradually, he became free of the phobia. Tomas is now happily married and enjoys all aspects of everyday life, including eating in public places.

Violence Experienced at Birth

When the infant's vulnerable brain is developing rapidly and its defenses are so immature, early imprints from trauma may actually be more deeply ingrained in the psyche than later imprints. They form a template, or a lens through which later events will be seen and evaluated. However, because of the generally accepted belief that babies are not conscious, violence at birth has often been accepted as part of standard operating medical procedure; it was not seen as violence. We normalized it! Thankfully, times have changed, and greater awareness has corrected outdated medical policies. However, the wounded descendants of the earlier times are now part of our population.

Here is a description of routine hospital birth procedures sent to me by a friend when he first began his practice as an obstetric doctor. He was well aware of the sensitivity of infants before and after birth.

The form of birth has taken a turn for the worse here in this city for mothers and babies. The only bright light is that when things get bad enough, the public will cry out. Meanwhile, there is much damage being perpetrated on unsuspecting mothers. The common behavior here: admit 38-40 weeks, break the bag of water, start Pitocin and epidural (at 2-3 cms) and push the Pitocin. When complete and with head at 1+ station, put on forceps, do a big episiotomy and pull the baby out. Dust the new infant off, clamp the cord right away, and hand the baby to the nurse who suctions him under bright lights on the resuscitation table, vigorously dries the baby, swaddles him, and then, if the doctor is finished sewing up the wound, gives the baby to the mother.

This kind of practice is a form of violence—violence both to the baby and the mother that can leave a legacy of mistrust and fear in our children. Such births may have become "normal," but they are light years away from what Nature intended.

In his 2002 book *Tomorrow's Baby,* Dr. Thomas Verny refers to early violence (or abuse) and the outcome in graphic terms: "The most severely exposed of our children are literally 'incubated in terror,' a process that permanently alters the brain. These damaged children enter a cycle of violence that passes from one generation to the next" p.195. Yes, these children grow up. They may become parents, and the cycle of violence is apt to be repeated. Fortunately, with research and books like Frederick LeBoyer's (1975) *Birth Without Violence* , there have been many positive changes.

In the past, many doctors and nurses were unaware of the psychological damage being done to mothers and babies. They were attuned to physical damage, but they did not see that many traditional medical practices were psychologically harmful. They did not consider these procedures from the viewpoint of the emotional pain felt by the baby, who is vulnerable, helpless, and exquisitely sensitive, both emotionally and physically. Long-term psychological damage was not a concern because the general perception was that there couldn't be any.

After years of working with clients to heal birth trauma, I know without any doubt that early violence contributes to a host of emotional and mental problems, whether perpetrated by an abuser or enacted unknowingly using the best of medical wisdom and technology. The infant may be harmed, especially at the time when attachment and bonding are critical, simply by unnecessarily separating the newborn from his mother.

Summing Up

When we see dysfunction in the life of an individual, we must ask what that individual's environment in the womb was like and whether the baby's first impressions were frightening and rejecting or loving and welcoming. These early impressions set a course, especially if they were traumatic.

The majority of children are able to thrive and lead fulfilling lives; however, other children who have been wounded in a variety of ways do not thrive. These are foster children, replacement children, abandoned children, runaways, children with physical pain and illnesses, and children left in "group homes" that resemble holding places. Many have been traumatized, ignored, abused, not seen, not valued, and not loved. They all need the same thing: love and support. Those words are easy to say, but to give love and support is sometimes difficult. Wounded humans of all ages need to be heard, seen, and kept safe by a compassionate adult or family. Some, like wounded animals may be "gun shy," angry, and mistrusting. Caring for them is not easy, and their caretakers will need support, too.

Lily, a hurt, neglected child, is now locked away for life. Who knows for sure what wounded her mother, Helen, or what the original source of Helen's trauma was. There is still hope that Megan will get the help she needs, but she won't if we pretend her trauma is over. Someday, someone will stumble over the unseen mass hidden "under the carpet of denial." Megan's trauma will be triggered, and she will overreact. We will wonder why someone went berserk and hurt her own child.

We must realize that in order to prevent future traumatic events rooted in violence, we must deal effectively with the emotional pain of our children wounded in the past, no matter their age, including our babies. Better yet would be to prevent the violence. Fortunately, for Megan, she had nurturing and loving adoptive parents.

Undoubtedly, insensitivity and a lack of education are responsible for creating "birth with violence." It is imperative for us to use our knowledge to educate parents and professionals, and to empower women to birth their babies in safe, peaceful, and loving ways. We must also work to educate and inform our legal, social, and political systems that would prefer, under the pressure of time and finances, to look away. If we want to reduce the violence in our homes, towns, and nation, we must begin at the beginning, in the womb and at birth or soon after—a time that contains our first lessons of trust or mistrust.

Now there is an opportunity to correct our attitudes and actions, to attempt to hit the mark, and to do it right! When parents and society do not recognize and correct the mistakes, they are handed down to the next generation.

Articles like the seemingly insignificant news release I read are a wakeup call that we are missing the mark. Not one of those little girls sinned. Helen, Lily, and Megan—each one reacted to what they had experienced, driven by unseen, unacknowledged pain from early childhood. Helen and Lily passed it down to the next generation. Fortunately, a potential exists for early trauma to be ameliorated by awareness and loving care. We hope Megan will be able to break the cycle.

12

Adoption:

Lingering Threads

Separation, isolation from, or abandonment by the caretaker is the greatest fear mammalian infants can experience.

JOSEPH CHILTON PEARCE

In search of my mother's garden, I found my own.

ALICE WALKER

Before there was a word for it, there was adoption. It is an ancient tradition. A Bible story tells us that Moses was discovered floating in a basket on the Nile and adopted by the Pharaoh's daughter. In ancient Rome, India, and China, and in pre-colonial America, people all used some form of adoption. The one common element has included the transfer of someone from one group, tribe, or culture to another. For the adoptee, it is a change, a shift of caregiver, even if the change occurs at birth.

When babies or young children are adopted, attention is usually focused on the adoptee's new environment. Too often the life lived in the watery world of the womb, the first environment, is not acknowledged as being relevant, as having sown seeds that will influence the later development of the adopted child. But neuroscience and research now reveal that in the early phases of the development of the brain, the fetus is learning to adapt to the biological mother's environment. Biology dictates that the developing fetus must respond to that environment to survive; thus, the human infant is not a blank slate when he arrives and breathes that first breath of air.

Every newborn at birth is approximately nine months old. Patterns have already been imprinted. Certain lessons about relating to others are learned in the womb, and these lessons must not be overlooked. If the infant has been loved and the biological mother's environment has been healthy and welcoming, seeds of trust have been sown. If the infant has been hated or unwanted, or if he has developed in an emotionally or physically toxic environment, seeds of fear will have been sown. Old wives tales across cultures have known this, and research is now linking psychological and physical vulnerabilities to pre- and perinatal life. What the biological mother experiences, the baby experiences.

When an infant is separated, temporarily or permanently, from his biological mother at birth, the infant is disconnected from all he has previously known as "home." Sometimes the separation occurs as the result of a routine hospital procedure that interferes with the natural bonding process of the mother and baby being together, skin to skin, after the baby's birth. Sometimes it occurs when the baby is born prematurely and is kept in an incubator for several weeks or months. Sometimes it occurs when the mother puts the child up for adoption, in which case the child may view adoption as an act of abandonment.

In some cases, separation from the biological mother may actually be advantageous to the infant after alienation has already occurred in the womb. Some women, due to their own birth history, abuse, or psychological problems, are not able to feel the intimacy of connection. They see their babies as an invasive threat, and the baby, responding to the toxic maternal environment in a defensive way, may psychologically wall himself off from the toxicity to stay separate from the dangerous negativity of his mother's world. (In such cases, there can be a cellular reaction and a spiritual separation that becomes the instigator of a fear response to life or emotions.)

However, regardless of how the separation occurs, there is a residue of pain, fear, and grief after any kind of loss, and the greater the loss, the greater the anxiety. The earlier the loss occurs, the deeper it is imprinted on the mind and body.

In the case of an adopted child, it is not helpful to deny the early loss and the need to mourn. Unfortunately, adoptive parents with the best of intentions may not want to acknowledge the power of the biological connection between the original mother and her baby, and it is common to hear the adopting mother deny any hint of her love not being just the same, as if she had given birth to the baby herself. However, regardless of the quality of her love, what is not factored in is that she is the second mother. The child's loss when the connection with the birth mother is severed is genuine. The child will unconsciously know it and feel it. To deny the loss is to deny the reality and hope of healing. What heals the pain of loss is a process of mourning and acceptance, supported by a loving family.

This chapter tells the stories of a fostered child and three adoptees and sheds light on how their experiences of separation from their birth mothers cast long-lasting shadows and sent ripples through their relationships and life choices.

Ted

One of the obstacles to opening the hard "crustacean" shell of an unbonded person is that person's repressed anger. In my office, Ted lay like a newborn infant with fists clenched, face red, and screaming in rage at his biological mother who had abandoned him at birth. He had been cared for by foster parents, but he said he had remained "an angry loner" and "felt cheated" for years. He had made it through college, married, and had a daughter, yet his rage frequently bubbled to the surface.

Now, in this therapeutic setting, his impotent infant rage was released. As his anger began to subside, he began to softly cry and call out to her, "Mama, Mama, Mama." I handed him a large, soft teddy bear that he hugged close to himself. He became very quiet and for several minutes lay peacefully hugging the toy. Tears began to flow again as he rocked back and forth. Much later, he said, "It's okay, I can love myself. I can love myself." Then with a large sigh, "I'm okay. I love myself. I can let her go now. I have loved . . . my heart feels so big and warm." He next described, as best as he was able, how he felt flooded with warmth, and light, and peace. He felt like some old chains had fallen away and that the world wasn't "gray" anymore.

When I saw him a few days later, Ted told me how he had talked to his friends more easily since our last session and how his old feeling of never belonging was less intense. He saw his two-year-old daughter as if he had never seen her before. How beautiful she was. He'd never been able to really be with her before. He had never known how much he loved his family. There was more work to do to integrate his new awareness into his life and to trust both his love and other people, but he knew he could never go back to his old way of living inside his shell. A butterfly once freed from the cocoon can never go back to it. A new cycle had begun.

Jerry

Jerry came to our STAR program because he needed time and support to deal with problems that had vexed him for some time. He knew that he had been adopted and reported that his parents were very loving. They had sent him to private schools and lavished him with all the possibilities of their wealth. At STAR, he was uncertain he could regress back to his birth and was surprised by what he uncovered when he did.

He learned that early in his mother's pregnancy, the womb was a comfortable place, but as he grew, he began to sense his mother's hostility. Jerry's environment was becoming toxic, and he wanted out! He said, "I jumped out because I had to get out! It was an unsafe place!" He was born two months premature.

We know that the blood from the mother supplies many things to the fetus, including the chemistry of her emotions. Frank Lake (1986), an eminent British doctor and surgeon in World War II and subsequently a psychiatrist who did pastoral counseling, recognized the umbilical effect as the "predominant mechanism" by which the mother transmits to the fetus her positive or negative emotional regard, or even her feelings of distress. According to Lake, the negative umbilical affect is "the source of much of the deepest adverse feeling and may be displaced somatically."

Bruce Lipton (2005) has explained that the cells of a fetus only have three options: to move toward, to move away from, or do nothing. Jerry's cells reacted, and he moved away from his mother by "jumping out" of the womb early. As a newborn, he lacked the cognitive skills to understand what was happening, but that did not mean his heightened senses were not reacting to the negative energies from his mother. The terror and pain overwhelmed his fragile existence! Separation, the antithesis of what a newborn needs, became his escape and his means of survival. To connect in any heartfelt way seemed to be dangerous and threatened his survival.

Usually an incubator is a terrifying and isolating place for a newborn; however, for Jerry, the connection with his biological mother's anger had been so toxic that being alone was a relief. He said, "The little glass box they put me into for quite some time was a very safe, warm place away from her." For Jerry, isolation in a box was preferable to being surrounded by his mother's hostility.

He later created an emotional psychological box that became his way of being in the world. As he explained it,

> I have spent my whole life inside a glass box covered by a one-way mirror from which others could get a lovely reflection of themselves and how wonderful they felt from me. I could see out. I lived in that box for forty-three years.

Jerry became an adaptive, compliant, people- pleasing child. He had first been rejected in the womb by his biological mother, and this rejection had left an imprint of abandonment. But he found a way to survive and stay safe and keep his emotional pain out of sight from everyone, including himself, by hiding his authentic self, adapting to others' expectations and needs, and reflecting back to them what they desired. He became a mirror. No one could really see him. He didn't even see who he was; he saw only his carefully constructed façade.

Through the years, friends tried unsuccessfully to reach him. He said,

> They would knock and knock, but I couldn't hear them because I was safe inside my box. If I let them in, they would see I was "not wanted" anyway. And they would go back home.

In the safe, nonjudgmental setting of therapy, Jerry was able to uncover and then release long-held primitive emotions he had held inside his body and in his unconscious since birth. In discovering a new range of choices for his life that were previously unknown to him, he was able to get out of the box. He found a new sense of freedom. He told me, "It is an amazing change. I can get out of the glass box! It's like giving a kid the most flawless gift they could ever have."

That was ten years ago, and he still lives outside the box. He has found a different career. He became involved in supporting the training of several young aspiring figure skaters. He also won a national gold medal in adult figure skating.

For Jerry, life has lightened up. Connecting no longer triggers his ancient fears of survival.

Karl

It was late, and the group room was almost empty when I noticed Karl curled up in a fetal position on a mat in the corner. He was clearly in a regressed state, sobbing his heart out. Something had triggered his emotions, and knowing he was in a safe situation and would not be abandoned, he had allowed himself to surrender to some painful old memories. Occasionally, he would reach out his arms and cry, "Mama." His crying had the deep sound of unbearable longing and pain.

Karl's story began soon after conception. His mother was having a secret affair and became pregnant. She was very upset and afraid to tell her husband. She did not want an abortion. For weeks, she agonized over what to do. Finally, she told her husband that she was pregnant and wanted to keep the baby. He was angry and told her that under no circumstances would he allow her to do that. Adoption was the only solution.

Fortunately, soon after his birth, a very loving couple adopted Karl. He had a safe, normal childhood with no abuse or neglect, and he loved his parents. But when he was in his teens, two events shattered his rather uneventful life and his carefully constructed persona. His beloved dog died, and shortly after that, his best friend committed suicide. The combination of these two losses triggered some deeper trauma, and Karl's emotional stability snapped. Heartbroken from the loss of his friend and his pet, Karl found himself overwhelmed and unable to cope. He fell apart and decided to run away.

For several years, Karl lived in the countryside as a wandering musician. Eventually, he returned to his hometown and enrolled in film school to become a cinematographer. When Karl joined my STAR group, his application to a prestigious, advanced film course had just been rejected. He was still playing music and working as an occasional medical photographer, and there had been a series of girlfriends, but Karl was never able to stay with anyone very long or make a serious commitment. He felt he was always searching for someone, yet no one felt right.

In therapy, he had the opportunity to release the unresolved grief from the losses of his friend and his beloved dog. He grieved those losses and surrendered to deep despair. As he sobbed and hugged himself and rocked back and forth, he also experienced an earlier unresolved and deeper loss—the loss of his biological mother.

Karl had never given much attention to his adoption. He had always known he had been adopted, but it seemed unimportant to him, and he was surprised when he found himself crying for his biological mother. He resisted facing that loss because he was afraid he would not be able to survive it. This fear probably corresponded closely to what he had felt as a helpless, frightened newborn.

Babies do experience loss and feel abandoned, and powerful feelings are overwhelming for them. With no intellectual understanding and limited physical abilities, one of the best survival defenses is to deaden those strong energies. As adults, they may try at all costs to block or avoid the feelings that surround the past trauma, since there is an unconscious fear that experiencing the emotions might restimulate the experience of the event itself. Actually, the trauma has already happened, and on one level, it was survived. As eminent British psychiatrist D. W. Winnicott (1989) said, "The breakdown which is feared is the breakdown that has already been" (p.129). However, the unconscious defense is to avoid anything that might restimulate the event. To the unconscious, time does not matter. Like a soldier at his post long after the war has ended, the unconscious stays on guard, and the intellect justifies and rationalizes the present behavior.

Karl's early trauma of being abandoned made it necessary that he always be on guard and never risk the possibility of another abandonment, and one way of doing that was to shun commitment. In such cases, the intellect can always find a reason why, such as "This person isn't right for me." But guarding against the dread of being abandoned drained Karl's energy and unconsciously ruled his life.

The deaths of his pet and his best friend breeched a defensive wall that had been in place since infancy. The resulting hurricane of emotions overwhelmed his normal ability to cope, and he experienced what is sometimes called a meltdown, a breakdown, or a falling apart. If allowed to be experienced, it can lead to a breakthrough.

During therapy, Karl skirted lightly around the circumstances surrounding his birth. He was visibly anxious when the subject came up.

We both knew that one day it would reveal itself, since clearly there was much more to process.

That time came when Karl was assisting in a STAR group. The memory of his birth was triggered like a volcanic eruption, and he lay curled up and sobbed. While I sat by him, he slowly uncurled his crumpled body and began tentatively in broken phrases to hit the mat and then slap his hands together like an angry, frustrated infant. Through his cries, he struggled to speak. He then whispered,

> I just wanted to touch her, to touch her, to complete—to touch her because my mind is not developing. She doesn't see me! She doesn't see me! She doesn't see me!

These shrieks were followed by a wailing cry and a jumble of words, as he continued to flap his arms and hands and kick his feet, just like an exasperated infant with no aim or focus.

> Why can't you have a baby in this world? What difference does it make about the father? Why can't you have me? What is wrong with the world?

Cultural standards, rigid norms, or right versus wrong might indeed be perplexing for the consciousness of a newborn. Where was the love and acceptance that biology had programmed Karl to expect? Where was the love his soul was created to receive and to give? One can only wonder what this tiny newborn learned of the ways of his new world. Was it an alien home for his soul?

In his regressed state, Karl continued in a muddle of hopelessness, frustration, and confusion, alternately crying out to "Mama" and to the world in general, as he angrily slapped the mat, the air, or himself. After a long time, he sat up and held his head in his hands. He moaned softly as he rocked back and forth, and finally said, "I saw everything. They are so frightened. This is not an ordinary birth—I see it!"

With the words "I see it," he became more agitated and slapped harder. There was an undeniable feeling of impotence and rage, all at once. Crying harder and rocking faster back and forth, he mumbled, "I want to say something to them, but they are so shut off from their feelings." The words sputtered out in cries and whispers. "So shut off! So shut off! Why can't they see?"

In time, I quietly asked, "What would you want to say to them, Karl?" After a long silence, he fell back on the mat and softly begged, "Just to take me up and put me. Put me. Put me on my mother's skin."

The basic primal desire must echo in all abandoned babies. "I need my mother's body. Put me on my mother's skin." Many times, I have suggested to the mother of a "difficult" baby that she hold the baby on her warm skin, for days if necessary. When the infant is placed skin to skin in the arms of a loving person, preferably the mother, survival responses melt away and are replaced by secure feelings of being safely rocked in a cradle of love.

Perhaps Karl was expressing some ancient wisdom of the biological collective, for he understood he needed some "completion" for his brain to develop properly. "I just wanted . . . to complete."

Again Karl dissolved into a waterfall of sobbing pain. Rocking and slapping himself lightly, he cried out,

> It's just up in their heads. Why can't they have me? Why can't they see the world? Why can't they see the world? She doesn't see the world because of her pain! And I don't! I don't see the world because of my pain.

At that, he collapsed back on the mat, curled up, and wept for a long time. The staff in the room and I were visibly moved, as we witnessed the agonizing heartbreak of this gentle and gifted young man. We also were equally moved by the transformation he underwent during this event. This session happened to be videotaped, and whenever I see the tape, I am deeply touched by the transparent wisdom of the infant's cries of "Why can't she have me?"

As Karl returned to the present time, he reached for my hand. Re-entry provides realization, insight, and integration. When we become consciously aware of the trauma and put it in the past, we understand that what was true in the past is no longer true in the present.

Karl began to connect his experiences to his life, and he realized why he was never able to maintain a relationship for a very long.

> I was looking for her [his mother's] touch. In all the girls I knew, I was looking for her touch. I was reaching out and calling for her, and she never came.

All mammals are designed to recognize their mothers, who protect their vulnerable offspring so they will survive. Just like ducks or lambs, a human infant knows his own mother. Everyone else is a substitute for the "real thing."

Of course, a substitute may be welcomed in the case of a very toxic mother, but the substitution is still a change recognized by the infant. This is not to imply that an infant will not accept and bond to someone other than his biological mother. It is simply a fact to be acknowledged.

A few months later, with the support of his adoptive family, Karl searched for his birth mother. He discovered that she worked at a café where he frequently ate. Their reunion went well, and Karl found some answers. He realized that his mother must have been in turmoil with feelings of guilt and sin, knowing her husband rejected the baby fathered by another man. There was no place for the baby in her family.

His birth mother told him that soon after his birth, she felt he was calling to her. She felt compelled to find him and to see him. When she asked the nurse to help her, she was told, "He has been taken to another hospital." She later found out that he had been there. Common policy at the time required that a mother not see or touch her baby when she had made the decision to give the child up for adoption. Perhaps the hospital feared that she might change her mind or experience an emotional awareness that would be too difficult for her. There was scant, if any, concern about what the baby might be feeling. Do babies feel? Karl did.

Often policy is counter to the natural needs of both the mother and the baby. I once met a midwife in England who told me that one day she entered a hospital nursery to find a young woman who was clutching her arms and silently weeping as she looked down at a baby in a bassinette. The midwife went up to her and asked what was wrong. Through her sniffles, the young mother said, "I want to hold my baby." The midwife replied, "Well, why don't you?" The answer she received was, "It is against hospital policy."

Fortunately, we are gradually becoming more aware and informed of issues surrounding adoption, attachment, and bonding. We better understand that the human needs of mother and baby might be more important than "policy." In *The Psychology of Birth* film, Dr. Marshall Klaus (2007) explains that

> the hospital practices that we've presently developed and we're using now for both mother and baby do not fit the physiology of either the mother or the baby. More hospitals are beginning to develop practices that do fit the physiology of mother and child.

About a year following his experience with STAR, Karl called me long distance on his birthday. Both of his mothers were with him, celebrating their son. There was enough love for all of them.

At forty, Karl's life took a dramatic turn. He entered medical school and is now working as a psychiatrist in a medical clinic. He told me he is disappointed that he is given so little time with each patient he sees— after all, he became a psychiatrist because of his concern and compassion for others. He realizes that people gave him the time he needed when he needed it, and he would like to return the gift to his patients; but once again, policy dictates otherwise and trumps human needs.

Annie

I first met Annie at Kenyon Ranch when she attended a ten- day STAR workshop. Annie was a tall, striking woman in her late twenty's. She was polite and had a tendency to isolate.

In reading her autobiography, a prerequisite for the workshop, I learned that she had been born in Korea and adopted by an educated couple from Minnesota, which is where she was raised. Her biological mother died shortly after Annie's birth. Her father, who was in deep grief, brought the baby girl home to be taken care of by an aunt. After her short stay, they took Annie to an orphanage for unwanted children and left her there until she was adopted. Four months later, she was adopted and living near the Canadian border.

Her American parents were attentive, kind, and responsible people. They had adopted two other children from Korea, so Annie had instant siblings, a younger brother and an older sister. However, Annie was a difficult child. She had temper tantrums and was very stubborn and hard to control. During those turbulent, growing-up years, Annie's parents tried to find professional help for her. Annie was intelligent and did well in school academically; however, social interaction was a struggle for her. She felt different and hated to even look at herself in the mirror.

Annie wrote a poem to express how she felt about her life.

Ugly Chinese Girl

Those words run through my head like a train,
again and again.
I'm not even Chinese.
I try to stuff the hurt back down
and hide it with a forced smile.
I walk down the unfriendly hall,
trying to remain unseen.
My legs are like Jell-O,
trembling under my imperfect body.
I thought that discrimination and prejudice were gone,
but it's clearly here,

lingering amidst the bursting halls.
I wish I could have large blue eyes,
not squinty brown ones,
just so I could reserve my feelings
and all my unsureness beneath
my ugly Chinese-girl smile.

She told me,

I started to believe there was something clinically wrong with me because of my race, and I shut out all things Asian, hoping it would make me Caucasian, and more likeable. I struggled with debilitating depression and continued to spiral downward, not only dealing with self-hatred, but also suffering from painful feelings of being unwanted and unloved by my birth family. I assumed that was why I was given up for adoption.

Annie came to STAR following a brief stay in a Denver hospital for depression. Her boyfriend had left her, and her beloved cat Chloe had died. Those two losses caused her to go into a deep, dark emotional place. Her parents were worried and consulted a therapist friend who suggested they send Annie to my STAR program. After several phone calls, it was decided.

Annie arrived at the ranch looking scared and exhausted. She showed very little interest in participating, but she did come to group sessions. Within a few days, she gradually settled in and became more involved in the process. The only strong feeling she had was grief for losing both her cat and her boyfriend, who was emotionally abusive. I asked her what Chloe meant to her, and she said, "Everything; she was my world."

One day, I handed her a stuffed teddy bear. She took it and held onto it, whimpering as she stroked it. When I took it away from her, she erupted into a towering rage and ran outside to a punching bag, picking up a plastic bat on the way. For thirty minutes, she yelled, hit, and kicked the bag nonstop. She needed no coaching from me. I stood nearby, simply watching. Exhausted, she eventually sat down and cried. Her release of anger and grief was a turning point in her therapy. For the remainder of the group session, she was involved and energized.

After the workshop ended, Annie returned to Denver. She decided to move to a warmer place and found a job and an apartment in Florida, not far from the beach. We kept in touch. She was still struggling, but she was taking action to reach out and make friends. She found a healthy physical outlet—long distance running—and made friends with others who also liked running. When meltdowns came, she sought support and was able to move through difficult times with more resilience. Annie was transforming herself.

Annie's story follows, in her own words.

I was born on June 6, 1983. My mother died three days later. She was twenty-four. The mother I never knew—somehow, I know she loved me. I grieve for her loss and feel it with every beat of my heart. She was six months pregnant with me when they found the cancer. I've lived with her sorrow all these years, not knowing what it was. Leukemia. I was almost fully developed. I was a new life when she was dying. Her body was deteriorating while I was growing stronger.

She fought for life, but in the end, she lost the battle and vanished from me. My heart aches at the thought of no memory of her. Though my brain doesn't remember, my heart does. It knows the pain of losing the person that gave me breath and life. I lose my breath when I think of how much it hurts.

For years, I pushed aside my Korean heritage. I wasn't proud of who I was and where I came from. It was difficult for me to accept myself in a world full of people who viewed me as different. Being different means you stand out in a crowd, and I was trying to fit in. I didn't want to face who I really was. I struggled for a long time with this, until finally I was able to loosen my grip on who I was and what I was to others. I no longer allowed others to define who I was. I began to see other Asian women as beautiful, whereas before I hadn't viewed them as role models of beauty. Then it dawned on me that I looked like them and that I could be beautiful, too.

I was finally allowing myself to be who I am and to become comfortable in my own skin. During this time, I became more curious about Korea and started to explore options for going back.

I'd gotten in contact with the adoption agency in Minnesota that processed my adoption and found out that they offered trips back to Korea every other year. As soon as I was able, I signed up for the next tour departing in July 2013. I knew the agency offered intermediary services to help find adoptees' families. I was finally ready to face whatever results would come from my own search for my roots. I knew there was a large chance I wouldn't be able to find anything, since I was older, and records were kept confidential to protect the privacy of the Korean families. I still wanted to try to find my birth father and birth brother, whom I had known about all my life. My heart was ready to open to this long lost, forgotten history of mine, and I was ready to own it. I made arrangements to go, and my American mother went with me.

One day I received a letter from my brother in Korea. It had been translated into English. "To my younger sister, whom I love," was how he started his letter to me after thirty years of not knowing each other. It brought me to my knees. I had not known if he knew about me. He was so young when I was adopted; I didn't know if anyone had told him. I had not grown up with a big brother. "Happy or sad, even though I am not by your side, I have always been with you. I always wanted to be with you." Words I didn't realize I needed to hear pulsed through my heart, and I finally started to open up to the sorrow of the loss of my big brother. I imagine two young children, walking hand in hand, brother and sister playfully bickering in Korean. We would have been close. I knew from the moment I met him that we would have been close.

The second letter I received was from my father. I learned that he had been searching for me for years. He called me his daughter. He called himself my father. He hadn't moved from the house he lived in when I was born, just in case I tried to find him. He expressed his sadness and guilt at letting me go. After thirty years, I didn't know him.

I tried to summon the emotions I was feeling when landing in Korea. I came up with nothing. For the majority of the trip, it was as if I was outside of myself, watching from somewhere else. It was so unreal that I was actually standing on the land where I was born, a world away from everything I knew, a world I didn't remember being in.

I knew I was in for many ups and downs, but for the time being, I was flatlining, acting almost like I was disinterested. Inside I was trying to come to grips with what was going on, the enormity of the situation at hand, and how long I had been waiting for it. I was for the first time in thirty years going to meet my family. In addition, I was standing on the soil I was from, and I was engulfed in the culture I never got to grow up in. I was seeing my homeland for the first time, tasting the flavors of my culture, and seeing others that look like me. I was no longer an anomaly in a sea of Caucasians, trying to find my place in the sun. It was a shock to the senses, not only being in a completely different environment, but also realizing it is my environment. It was a whole other level of awe and disbelief. This place held my roots, my history, my family, and I had finally gathered enough courage to come back to the place that had sent me away.

My brother met my mother and me at the airport. It was strange, but we recognized each other immediately.

Later, my brother and I were sitting next to each other at dinner. A waitress came over and pointed to us and said we looked like each other. It was amazing to hear it being said out loud. I looked like my brother. After all these years, people could still tell we were family.

My birth brother and I went together to the temple where Umma, my birth mother, is taken care of. This was the first time her two children paid their respects together. [It is] something I will hold dear forever. Side by side, brother and sister finally together with their Umma.

I saw the hospital where I was born, where my birth mother lived during the last month of her life. I saw the place where I was brought into the world. The same place my birth mother passed away. Breathless.

On the day my birth mother had her last rites read to her, she and my birth father made a decision to give me up for adoption. I would never grow up with the brother who was only sixteen months older than I was. They had planned my birth so that we would be close in age.

How strange it is to think of how different life would be if she had lived. When I lost my mother, I lost my family, my culture, my heritage, my history, my language, my country. Finally, I was able to deal with the sadness of these losses and reclaim them for my own.

When I met my father, I went over to him and hugged him. Koreans don't traditionally hug when greeting each other, but he hugged me back. All the air sucked out of my lungs, and I went mute. I couldn't comprehend what was happening.

My birth father said that I am like my mother. She was expressive and exuberant and stubborn and willful and sensitive and loving. Like me. I am like her. I have her spirit. He loved her. He still does. She lives through me.

Every day I think of her. And every day I know she is with me. I can feel shadows of her grace in the sunrise and sunset. How deeply I wish I could see her with my own eyes, feel her embrace on my skin, and hear her voice, her laughter, her heartbeat. Through these tears, I find strength. I know that she loved me fiercely, and I'm grateful.

Umma, I love you. Umma, I miss you. I thank you for giving me this beautiful life and the strength to persevere. I thank you for giving me the ability to love with all my heart. I will hold you enveloped in my heart forever, right where you belong.

Later, my brother told me his struggles while growing up without a mother. He had a lot of anger and sorrow from his own childhood. I told him my family had known that when I was adopted I had an older brother, and they said that if he was ever placed for adoption, they would like to adopt him. He told me he wished that it had happened. My heart twisted in my chest. I realized then how the immense pain from our mother's death was rippling through him, too.

He told me that right after my birth, things were hard in Korea, but if my birth family had held out for just a little longer, they would have been able to keep me. I see the look in his eyes when he says this. I can see the grief of losing his sister and the wish to have grown up with me, his only sibling from Umma.

I was lucky that I got to spend a lot of time with him during my short trip to Korea. My brother is funny, kind, thoughtful, and giving. I told him my favorite treat from Korea was melon bars, and he surprised me with one the next time I saw him. He'd refused to go on a blind date before I visited, because he did not want to be distracted when I was there. He held the umbrella over my head when it rained. He posed for silly pictures with me. He took me to see the town where our Umma grew up. He was the best big brother I could have ever asked for. He still is.

He came to the airport to say goodbye on the day I left Korea. He sat with me, and we drank orange juice together. It was the best orange juice I ever had. He promised me he would try his hardest to be a good big brother, and that he wanted to make me proud. I told him I was already proud. He walked me to the gate, and he couldn't go any further. I hugged him one last time. He told me not to cry. I couldn't help it. The moment came when I had to let go. I let go. I kept walking. I watched him waving goodbye until the wall blocked my view. My Oppa. My big brother, I love him so much. And I know he loves me, too.

My language, something that should be second nature to me, is a foreign entity floating above my head. I try to catch it, but each time it bobs upward and away just out of my reach. I am scrambling to learn, but can't help but feel frustration at having to learn my native language at the age of thirty. Shouldn't I just know it?

My culture, the way people eat, what they eat, the gestures, the customs, the history, the people, the clothing—all of it so rich and filled with practiced traditions. It's beautiful, but I was like a bumbling idiot when trying to participate. It was awkward to do a traditional bow, and someone had to hold me up so I wouldn't plant my face on the floor. I couldn't keep my legs a pretzel shape for longer than five minutes, and I had to stretch them out at the dinner table, one of the rudest gestures in Korea while eating. The beautiful hanbok (traditional Korean garment) my birth father bought me looked more like a costume on me than a tradition. I wasn't playing dress-up; I was genuinely trying to fit in, to claim my place in my culture. But there, in my home country, I am different. I am American, but I am Korean. No, I am American. No, I am Korean. Who am I?

I blamed myself for so many years, but I have come to learn that it's not my fault. It's also not my birth family's fault. I know they gave me the best chance at life by choosing adoption. It's no one's fault. It just is.

The beliefs I had about myself that I wasn't good enough or worthy of love went so deep that they became a part of my programming. I ran away when things got tough. I sabotaged relationships. I didn't believe in myself.

Now I am working to undo them, because I don't want to live my life in fear. Because I am worthy of a life filled with love. Sometimes, the days can be unbearable, when the battle seems to be about how to take the next step. My eyes dull out. And I stare at nothing. I have had many screaming matches with Spirit, insisting that I'm not strong enough to get through this. But I am still alive. I am not dead. And I stay with my pain instead of running from it. I allow it to come, so I can release it and make room for love.

And I know the truth now. I asked my dear Oppa if he loves me. If my Appa still loves me. The answer was yes to both questions, and they told me I am always in their thoughts. So I take that in and begin to let go of the story I was telling myself, because that story is not true. It never was.

It's a process, but I'm hanging in. I must practice patience with myself and above all, love.

In working with Annie over these last few years, I have witnessed a transformation. When I first met her, she hated herself and was very ill at ease in the world. Where did she fit in? Would she ever?

Today, Annie has many friends who love her and fill her social calendar. Her vitality is enhanced by her current commitment to long distance running and the warm group of friends with whom she shares the sport. She has a demanding job in human resources with too much pressure, but she is learning to speak up for herself. She has an engaging and full life.

I believe therapy empowered her and gave her self-esteem and gratitude for life. She grieved the loss of her mother and began to understand how damaging that loss had been to her. She had an opportunity to return to Korea and met her biological family. Her experience in the land of her birth was profound.

Her relationship with her American family has become even closer. She loves each of her families and maintains a close connection with them.

As for me, I am grateful that I have become much more sensitive to the importance of acknowledging culture and its lasting influence. Annie's discussion of this influence is revealing.

I am lucky to say that my adoptive family has been so wonderful, and raised me with so much love and kindness. The memories I have of growing up, of many moments, can never be taken away from me. My parents really made an effort to acknowledge my Korean heritage and would cook traditional Korean meals for us at home. As for me, it took a very long time to accept that as being a part of me. I was fully entrenched in my parents' European background, and comfort food to me was meat and potatoes. It still is, although now I have embraced and honor the Korean side of myself.

Through therapy and intense inner work, I have reached a point where I can embrace my American and Korean cultures as my own. I am not one or the other, and I find a lot of peace in not having to choose between the two.

Both of my families love me an incredible amount, and I am finally able to accept and let in the love I have always wanted and deserve from them. And for that, I am forever grateful.

I do not wish my life to be any different. This journey is my own, and this is my story. This is who I am. I've learned the power of love and that it never ceases. Even when I'd given up, it was still there, flickering in the darkness. I've learned to call upon myself for strength, and I've learned how to find it. I've learned that anger is a mask for deep sadness, and that running away from it means it only follows you through life that much longer. I've learned how to let go and trust in my own journey. I've learned to take chances and jump, because now I can fly. I've learned compassion at the deepest level. I want others walking the same kind of path as me to know they are not alone. I am profoundly lucky to have loving supportive parents who have stood by me through every trial and triumph in my lifetime.

My heart is open, and I stand with my feet planted firmly on the ground. I will rise again to dance among the flames of my heart. And I'm dancing!

Summing Up

To give a child a safe home is a blessing. But to separate an infant from his original mother usually causes pain and anxiety. In Karl's case, we are struck with the profound wisdom of his words: "Why can't they have me?" Perhaps we need to wonder with what consciousness he was seeing. Are we so shut off from our feelings, the realm of the heart, and the domain of the right hemisphere, that we do not see? In the eyes of Mother Nature, all children are blessed and welcome.

In Karl's case, the two painful and shocking losses of his best friend and his pet dog broke the dam that held in his earlier grief. As a newborn, the pain of the loss of his mother had overwhelmed him. Without having the ability to comprehend why she had disappeared, he was unable to process his feelings. Repression was an effective defense when faced with debilitating and disorganized rage, confusion, and emotional pain. However, emotional repression does not eliminate those feelings. They may slumber, but they do not die. When the brain is not able to, or supported in, processing the trauma, the body behavior expresses it.

The adult has options both physically and mentally that a newborn lacks. As an infant, Karl instinctively sought survival in burying the overwhelming pain. As a teenager, his old pain fueled his angst, and his solution was to run away. One can run to a new location, but emotions and personal history go along.

The teen years with dramatic hormonal changes are often a time when repressed or denied feelings break through, triggered by a present-day dramatic event. Old emotions rush forward to intensify present-day feelings. Together, they may form a firestorm. The intensity of the firestorm takes on qualities of extreme life and death traumas. To the newborn, the trauma felt that way.

Unrecognized as partly from the past, these old emotions are projected and acted out in present time. The individual does not remember anything of what he has forgotten or repressed. He reproduces it not as a memory but as an action. He repeats it without knowing that he is repeating an old trauma. In effect, the acting out is a way of remembering. However, even when this dynamic is understood, rarely are pre- and perinatal roots of the problem explored and resolved. The cycle becomes repetitive, as repression and occasional explosions continue.

To heal early traumas, we must recognize that the sensory world of the infant does not begin at birth. There is a radical change with regard to stimulation of sensory receptors between the prenatal and postnatal worlds, but birth brings an extension and intensification. Birth—perhaps the greatest change or matrix shift any human being experiences before death—is a gateway, part of a continuing path. If an infant developed in a womb of love, there will be less anxiety and more trust than if a child was rejected, in which case the child will be born with fear and mistrust. According to Erik Erickson (1980), the first foundational lesson we learn is to either trust or mistrust. This lesson is embedded in an adoptee's life, just as it is in any other infant's life.

What happens next after leaving the biological mother's womb is critical, just as life during gestation is critically important for the physical and psychological well-being of the infant. Perhaps the most elementary mammalian need is to be held in the arms of a loving caregiver to develop a sense of secure attachment. Sadly, too often this does not occur.

In my longtime practice, I have worked with many clients who were adoptees. Their journeys have ranged from those who chose to find their biological mother, to others who did not believe their adoption had any bearing on their current problems and had no desire to explore it or trace their biological family trees. Some clients feared the adoptive mother would be upset and chose to drop the subject.

Most were born when their mothers were shunned, sent away, sometimes even disowned or abandoned because they were pregnant and unmarried. Many grew up not knowing they had been relinquished at birth. One client found her adoption documents among her adoptive mother's papers after her death. Several found out when the truth was flung at them like an angry knife when they misbehaved.

Fortunately, adoption has "come out of the closet," as has the stigma attached to unmarried pregnant women. We longer send unmarried pregnant mothers away to some distant place to "cover up the disgrace," and we no longer lie to adopted children.

Often, adoptees' adoptive mothers support the search, which may or may not result in the hoped-for resolution. One client who found her birth mother was angrily rejected and ended up retraumatized by the experience. Her early grief and anger erupted, and in all of her yearning, she demanded to be accepted by her biological mother. Her dreams and years of idealizing her "real mother" splintered into shards of grief and rage. The situation only worsened with threats of a restraining order by her biological mother.

In a more positive vein, many reunions leave adoptees filled with appreciation and gratitude for their adoptive family as well as with a warm relationship with their biological family. They are lovingly embraced by their biological siblings and their biological parents, and they maintain good relationships with both.

Separations are part of life, and they can be transforming or traumatic. Their gift can be resiliency and confidence, but to deny the loss is to deny the reality and hope of healing.

13

Trailing Clouds of Glory:
Awakening to Our Divine Source

In *The Radiant Child*, Thomas Armstrong wrote, "There is a hidden side of childhood that needs to be acknowledged as a valid dimension of the child's existence over and above what is easily observable"(Armstrong, 1985, p.3). Armstrong maintained there is "a hidden line of maturation that describes the growth of the infant 'from the spirit down,' by this I mean there is a part of the child, which does not have its roots in the mother or earth matrix . . . A Zen koan asks, 'What was your original face, the one you had before your parents were born?'" (p.3). The implication is that our beginning was not our birth; rather, birth is a point on a continuum. We came from elsewhere. As the poet William Wordsworth (1967) wrote,

> Behold the Child among his new-born blisses . . .
> See, at his feet, some little plan or chart,
> Some fragment from his dream of human life,
> Shaped by himself with newly-learnèd art . . ." (p.181).

Unfortunately, when pre- or perinatal trauma occurs and affects the brain's development, a common defense is to disassociate from the soul. Later in life, in the process of surviving physically, we often forget our souls, our purpose, and our oneness with our creator. The vulnerable and innocent open heart is often the object of the disassociation. A false sense of self, a persona, or mask, is created to protect that open heart, but seeing through its eyes, we do not see clearly. As Antoine de Saint-Exupery (1943) wrote in his classic book *The Little Prince*, "It is only with the heart that one can see rightly; what is essential is invisible to the eye."

For the most part, we are content to believe that living with a false sense of self, a restricted self, is our only option. Like circus animals, we live in our restricted but safe cages, now familiar to us, and we relate comfortably to others who are likewise caged. We feel "normal." We buy the restricted existence, but at the risk of becoming terminally normal. Anything that does not fit into the box, we label "abnormal," including genuine mystical experiences. When I remember William Wordsworth's (1804) famous lines "Shades of the prison-house begin to close/Upon the growing Boy," I think of my many clients who have felt closed down and bound by rigid rules and beliefs and by their pain.

Recall Jung's (1963) central question, "Are we related to something infinite or not?" Implicit here is the view that man is a spiritual being and that transformation is possible. Some individuals who disassociate from their souls are uncomfortable in their own skins, and they ask, "Who am I?" The question can be gnawing, yet it can also be explored with courage and grace.

Deborah

Deborah was in her late thirties when she came to a workshop I was leading. Her intelligence was evident, though she was quite reserved and resistant to my suggestions. She was a descendant from an aristocratic family in Brazil, and as a college graduate, she had spent time working in the environmental movement. Now, she was struggling with alcoholism and searching for meaning in her life.

Her birth had been very traumatic. In fact, she was born dead and resuscitated by the doctors at the hospital. She said, "They told me I was blue and not breathing, but they soon got my breathing going." The same trauma had happened to both of her older sisters.

In the course of Deborah's therapy, we often visited her birth. She told me how she remembered hovering above her body, looking down at it, and coming close. The closer she got, the more terrified she became. "I would zoom away. I didn't want to be part of that body."

Actually, Deborah was uncomfortable with more than her body; she was uncomfortable with her life. She found alcohol gave her an escape from her continual struggle to be present. She had recurring nightmares about hanging within a deep crack in the ground, each hand clinging to one side, neither one strong enough to lift her up, but at the same time, she was terrified to let go lest she fall into the abyss below. So she hung suspended between life and death.

Deborah was a restless spirit, and often she was not grounded in her body. She was ambivalent about being present and leading an unfulfilling life. I felt her dream was a metaphor for the way she felt about life. She clearly had a body, but much of the time she was not fully in it. She spent most of her time "peeking into" life or becoming involved in some public activity and then quickly running away from it. She attended school and followed her routines precisely, pretending to be "like everyone else." Her heart was split between two worlds, the world of spirit and the world of matter.

Laura

A bright, young lawyer in her thirties, Laura arrived at Pocket Sanctuary to attend a workshop scheduled to last three weeks. Her gracious, charming manner and her southern accent quickly revealed her background and culture, yet her lovely demeanor actually disguised her inner, fragile reality. All was not well in Laura's life. Laura's initial report disclosed she had already battled through several rounds of cancer.

This would have been ample reason for the despair that brought her to the workshop. However, she further described in her biography that many times in her life she had deep inner feelings of loss and hopelessness; she felt as if she didn't "belong." The words "I just don't feel real" quickly caught my attention. She hoped to uncover the source of these feelings. For years she had been thinking, "What's wrong with me? I have everything, so what am I missing? What is this emptiness I feel?"

During the three-week program, I worked individually with Laura a number of times. One day she asked me to do a birth regression with her, so we set it up. Two other staff members and I arranged the room with mats, pillows, a blanket, bottled water, and Kleenex—the usual provisions found in a therapy room. To ensure Laura felt comfortable, I asked if there was anything else she wanted to have at her disposal. She said, "Yes, I would like a scarf to cover my eyes." I retrieved a black scarf from the back of a chair, and I asked if it would work for her. She nodded yes, and I proceeded to lightly fold it and then hand it to her. She adjusted and readjusted the scarf on her head and face until she was satisfied that the dark triangle of cloth rested point down over her face. She was then ready to begin the regression.

The three of us sat around her with our customary attitude of quiet reverence and respect. Slowly, as I spoke relaxing and soothing words, Laura's breathing became gentle and even. She drifted farther into a calm, interior place. Next, I softly suggested she imagine becoming smaller and smaller until she was floating in a warm, watery world. Her breathing was rhythmic and easy. Shortly, she rolled over on her side and curled up her legs. Within a few minutes, Laura began to squirm, and her breathing became labored, as if she were struggling to get oxygen. I was startled when she took a deep gasping breath, lunged forward, and let out a long exhale. Then she returned to her earlier position stretched out on the mat and rested motionless. Her breathing resumed a normal, quiet cadence. We maintained a silent presence with her. I sensed she had reached another level of consciousness. It felt to me as if she were somewhere beyond us in another time and space.

After what seemed like a long time, Laura began to mutter quietly. As her whispering continued, she raised both hands and moved them as if she were patting down or smoothing out something. She kept flattening some invisible object—invisible at least to me, but not to Laura.

Gradually, her sounds began to form words. I leaned closer toward her to hear what she was saying. In fact, the support team leaned forward, too. This is what we heard: "I have come to the land of the flat people. I have come to the land of the flat people." Over and over she repeated the words, as if they were a mantra. Abruptly, her tone changed, and in a more decisive way, she declared, "I will be flat, too."

Her words were the only sound in the room, her hands the only movement as they continued to flatten something in her world that was clearly real to her but that was unseen by us. Next, Laura lay still without speaking for a long time. We waited. Finally, she said faintly, "I have come to the land of the dead people." After another long pause, she folded her hands and rested them on her stomach. She took a deep sigh and said, "I will be dead now." The deafening silence in the room gave me a chill.

A little while later, she began to stir and removed the scarf. She opened her eyes and looked around the room. I knew that in her own time, she would share her journey with us or she would not. Often transpersonal experiences need to be told. In other cases, there aren't any words to adequately convey the experience. The person who takes the journey makes that decision.

After several days, Laura shared with me that her regression was extremely healing for her. Her feelings of inadequacy and harsh self-criticism had finally been replaced with feeling "at home" and at peace with herself. Perhaps Laura had arrived at the place British psychologist Harry Guntrip (1968) refers to as the "lost heart of the self." She realized that she was not a "flat person" and that she had never been able to become one.

After a considerable amount of time, I was still pondering over the words Laura had spoken in her regression when I turned to a passage of Jung's (1961):

> For thousands of years, rites of initiation have been teaching rebirth from the spirit; yet strangely enough, man forgets again and again the meaning of divine procreation... It is easy enough to drive the spirit out of the door, but when we have done so the salt has lost its savour (p.783).

Historically, salt has been used to confirm a person's worth. Salt was so valuable that Roman soldiers were paid with it. In contemporary times, we speak positively of a person as being "the salt of the earth," meaning a good person, honorable, and trustworthy. In contrast, when a person is dishonorable and untrustworthy, we deem that person "not worth his salt." Possibly, the words Laura whispered over and over referred to some absence of spirit she saw lacking in "the flat people." The saltiness of their spirit had been driven out.

Several months later, a friend of Laura's called to say she had peacefully passed away. I was drawn to Donald Kalsched's (2013) words in *Trauma and Soul*: "There remains within us a part of the original oneness that longs to return to that great spiritual reality from which we came and about which we have forgotten. This splinter of the divine radiance we call the soul."

Summing Up

Individuals like Deborah seem to the majority of us to be difficult to be with or "not really present." They may become daydreamers, mystics, or saints, or they may be locked away in mental hospitals. They can also become alcoholics or great pretenders and fool not only others but also themselves. They seem to be stuck being in and yet not of the world, peering over a gate that has rusted shut. They feel the safest when they are alone because they are never truly comfortable with people.

Like Deborah, many other people who have experienced early traumas close down. They shrink, harden, or restrict their hearts in an effort to protect themselves from the overwhelming pain they experienced. But when our hearts are closed, we are separated from the awareness of our souls and from our own innermost wisdom and natural knowing.

Unfortunately, this closing down began before these individuals took their first breath. For others, it came later, when they saw the hypocrisy between the words and actions of those around them or after they tried to find their heart by mirroring responses to their love and finally gave up.

Childhoods are cluttered with events that diminish our ability to love and trust. Naturally, we close down. Longfellow (1847) wrote, "When the heart goes before, like a lamp and illumines the pathway, many things are made clear, that else lie hidden in darkness." With a closed heart, the Spirit within us is dim at best, and it is difficult for us to find our authenticity.

But much like a tiny splinter annoys us, our soul has the power to awaken us to our divine source in spite of our attempts to deny or ban it from our awareness. Other times, it makes itself known in an epiphany or flash of intuition or clear seeing or an overwhelming feeling of peace or love, which may feel like a miracle.

In my work around pre- and perinatal issues, I have held the hands of individuals seeking to find their authentic self. They rarely say it is longing for a soul that motivated them to come in for therapy. Yet in the process of regressing back in time, they often find the gate wide open and tumble through into the arms of love. They also sometimes find their soul during a crisis or when they experience an epiphany or a flash of insight or an overwhelming feeling of peace and love.

Fortunately, it is never too late to begin the process of healing. Wordsworth (1804) reminded us of this when he wrote of the awakening of the child:

But he beholds the light, and whence it flows,
He sees it in his joy…

During her final illness, when Lady Nancy Astor (1981) awoke to find all her children assembled at her bedside, she asked her son, "Jakie, am I dying, or is this my birthday?" He answered, "A bit of both."

Therapy is also a bit of both. To grow and expand our consciousness, our old habitual patterns of thinking, feeling, and behaving must die. Those deaths are often experienced with a great deal of fear. After all, we originally learned those patterns as ways of surviving and getting our needs met or as methods of adapting to abusive and threatening situations, chosen as the best way of coping in our unique situation. Then, as we go along, we learn to justify our early patterns, and in a very real sense we become addicted to them. Out of fear they were born, yet out of love they can die. With their demise, there is space and opportunity to see the present clearly and to "be born again" into new ways of being. Love always heals, but one's heart has to be open enough to be able to receive it. The presence of fear makes that difficult or seemingly impossible. I believe therapy is one way to open the heart to love.

Afterword

Womb Prints by Barbara Findeisen, MS, MFT, is a profoundly important contribution toward healing societal dysfunction and ensuring the healthy development of future generations. Findeisen is an internationally recognized pioneer and leader in the field of prenatal and perinatal psychology, as well as the founder of STAR (Self-Analysis Toward Awareness Rebirth). The STAR process focuses on the influence of prenatal and perinatal environments as the source of adult psychological problems. Through behavioral reprogramming modalities, the information acquired in this process has been used to transform thousands of lives.

In *Womb Prints*, Findeisen reviews the profound impact that the prenatal and perinatal period has on the health and fate of a developing child. She provides a compilation of personal and patient experiences that illuminate how patterns of thoughts, emotions, and actions that shape our lives are fundamentally programmed in our earliest developmental experiences. The important conclusions are soundly based on the most recent advances in genetics, neuroscience, psychology, and spirituality.

For example, it was once thought that genes were hereditary programs that primarily provided our physical, emotional, and behavioral characteristics and that our genes are inherited in a random fashion from our mother's and father's genomes. This conclusion leads to the belief that genes fundamentally determine our fate. Hence, we are left with the perception that we are powerless "victims" of our heredity.

In 1990, the revolutionary new field of epigenetics introduced a profoundly different reality. Before this time, it was thought that genes were "self-actualizing," that they were able to turn themselves on and off. This assumption is now recognized to be completely false; genes do not control their own activity. Unfortunately, this misunderstanding led to the notion of genetic determinism, the belief that genes "control" biology and our fate.

In contrast, epigenetic science emphasizes that signals from the environment, especially those sent to the cells via the blood and nervous system, regulate gene activity and can even rewrite the information encoded in our genome. The primary gene-regulatory "signals" are derived from the chemistry and energetic vibrations released by the brain in response to the mind's "perception" of the environment. For example, a mind perceiving love causes the brain to release, among other neurosecretions, dopamine (offers a sense of pleasure), oxytocin (supports bonding with the source of pleasure), and growth hormone (enhances the body's vitality). The signals released by the nervous system in a state of love encourage psychological contentment and enhance physical health.

In contrast, a mind experiencing fear releases hormones (e.g., cortisol) and inflammatory agents that collectively shut down the body's growth and maintenance systems and inhibits the function of the immune system. Fear results in distress, a condition that is now recognized to be the leading cause of disease.

Genetic determinism implies that the development and fate of an individual is encoded in the genes, and it restricts the mother's role in the development to simply providing good nutrition. Prior to epigenetic science, medical practitioners primarily focused on the nutritional contributions of the mother's blood in nourishing the fetus. Epigenetic mechanisms now focus attention on neuro-regulatory information signals used to adjust the mother's physiology and behavior in response to her perception of the environment. These regulatory signals cross the placenta and directly shape fetal gene activity and behavior. Through this pathway, the developing child senses and responds to the environment that the mother experiences.

Human behavioral characteristics cannot be preprogrammed in the genes simply because the demands of the environment and the behaviors of culture are continuously evolving. Isolated in the watery world of the womb, a fetus is disconnected from the surrounding environment.

However, the mother's perception of the world is translated by her nervous system into blood and nerve-borne hormones and emotional chemicals that adapt her biology to survive in the world she experiences. These maternal regulatory signals are transported across the placental barrier and directly impact the genetics and behavioral programming of the developing fetus.

Consequently, Nature designed the mother to be a child's "head start program" by providing environmental information that will enable her child to enhance its survival by adapting its genetics and behavior to conform to the world into which it will be born. Simply, the mother and the father (his actions impact the mother's perception of life) are "genetic engineers" whose perceptions and actions shape their child's behavior and future health.

A developing child's brain does not express self-consciousness as a predominant neural activity until it acquires alpha EEG frequencies around seven years of age. Before age seven, the brain primarily operates in the lower theta EEG frequencies, which represent a state of hypnosis. This is the sensitive period wherein a fetus or child responds to the exigencies of the environment and unconsciously downloads life experiences.

For over a decade, medical research has recognized that "environmental processes influencing the propensity to disease in adulthood operate during the peri-conceptual, fetal and infant phases of life." (P. D. Gluckman & M. A. Hanson, 2004, *Science* vol. 305[1733]). Epigenetic insights now reveal the pathway by which parental attitudes, emotions, and behaviors are translated into chemical and energetic signals that cross the placental barrier and "program" the genetic activity of a developing fetus. In addition to having an impact on health, womb experiences have also been shown to shape the character of the nervous system and lay the groundwork for personality, emotional temperament, and the power of higher thought.

In the light of epigenetics, the importance of prenatal life experiences is significantly greater than previously thought. *Womb Prints* is an invaluable resource that illuminates the fundamental patterns by which womb experiences influence the appearance of specific disease and behavioral dysfunctions in later life.

Through an assessment of developmental anomalies experienced during gestation and the birth process, therapists, medical clinicians, and the general audience are provided important insights into the origin of deviant adult behaviors.

Womb Prints is a groundbreaking contribution that defines how prenatal and perinatal experiences generate a biological template that can color subsequent feelings and attitudes about our relationships and ourselves. Findeisen's clinical studies, in conjunction with the extensive information provided in her patient case histories, contributes insights into resolving adult behavioral issues. More importantly, these studies will encourage mothers and fathers to engage in conscious parenting techniques behaviors that create supportive environments in which their children can express their highest potential.

Bruce H. Lipton, PhD, Stem cell biologist
and bestselling author of
The Biology of Belief, Spontaneous Evolution,
and *The Honeymoon Effect.*

References

Antonella, M.C. (2015). *Perinatal programing of neurodevelopment.* New York: Springer.

Armstrong, T. (1985). *The Radiant Child.* Wheaton, IL: Quest Books.

Bacon, F. (2012). General Preface. *The Philosophical Works of Francis Bacon.* New York: Rare Book Club.

Barr, P. (1989). Pre and perinatal loss. APPPAH International Congress, Amherst, Ma, August, 1989. See also: *Stillbirth & newborn death: Death & life are the same mystery.* New South Wales: Sands. 1987.

Centers for Disease Control and Prevention. (n.d.). National health and nutrition examination survey (NHANES). National Institutes of Mental Health. Retrieved from https://www.nimh.nih.gov/health/statistics/prevalence/any-disorder-among-children.shtml.

Chamberlain, D. (1995). What babies are teaching us about violence. *Pre- and Perinatal Psychology Journal, 10*(2), 57-74.

Chamberlain, D. (1998). *The Mind of Your Newborn Baby.* 3rd ed. Berkeley, CA: North Atlantic Books.

Chamberlain, D. (2013). *Windows to the womb: Revealing the conscious baby from conception to birth.* 1st ed. Berkeley, CA: North Atlantic Books.

Cummings, e. e. (1938). *Collected Poems.* New York: Harcourt, Brace.

deMause, L. (1982). *Foundations of Psychohistory.* 1st ed. New York: Creative Roots.

Erikson, E. H. (1980). *Identity and the Life Cycle.* New York: W. W. Norton.

Ewing, C.P. (1997). *Fatal families: The dynamics of intrafamilial homicide.* Thousand Oaks, CA: Sage.

Freud, S. & Breuer, J. (1895/2000). *Studies in Hysteria.* New York: Basic Books.

Guntrip, H. (1969). *Schizoid phenomena, Object relations and the self.* 1st ed. London: International Universities Press.

References

Haarer, J. (1934). *The German Mother and Her First Child.* Munich: J. F. Lehmann.

Hayton, A. (2010). Carrying a single twin: Breaking the silence to reduce stress. *Journal of prenatal and perinatal psychology and health, 25*(1), 33-43.

Herman, L.G. (2013). *Future primal: How our wilderness origins show us the way forward.* Novato, CA: New World Library.

Hull, W. (1986). Psychological treatment of birth trauma with age regression and its relationship to chemical dependency. *Pre- and Perinatal Psychology Journal, 1*(2), 111-135.

Hüther, G. (2013). *Approaching humankind: Towards an intercultural humanism.* Edited by Jörn Rüsen. Taipei: National Taiwan University Press.

Hüther, G., & Kohn, M.H. (2006). *The Compassionate Brain: How Empathy Creates Intelligence.* Durban, South Africa: Trumpeter.

Ingraham, C. (2014). Our infant mortality rate is a national embarrassment. *Washington Post, September 29.*

Janov, A. (2011). *Life Before Birth: The Hidden Script That Rules Our Lives.* Chicago: NTI Upstream.

Janus, L. (1997). *The Enduring Effects of Prenatal Experience– Echoes from the Womb.* Northvale, NJ: Jason Aronson.

Jung, C. (1961). *Freud & Psychoanalysis.* Vol. 4 of *Collected Works of C. G. Jung.* Princeton, NJ: Princeton University Press.

Jung, C. (1963). *Memories, Dreams, Reflections.* New York: Pantheon.

Kalsched, D. (2013). *Trauma and the soul: A psycho-spiritual approach to human development and its interruption.* 1st ed. New York: Rutledge Press.

Karr-Morse, R., & Wiley, M.S. (1998). *Ghosts from the nursery: Tracing the roots of violence.* New York: Atlantic Monthly Press.

Klaus, M. (2004). *The psychology of birth* DVD. Distributed through Owl Productions, http://owl.postle.net/birth

Korbin, J.E. (2003). Children, Childhoods, and Violence. *Annual Review of Anthropology, 32,* 431-436.

Lake, F. (1966). *Clinical theology, A theological and psychiatric basis to clinical pastoral care.* London: Darton, Longman, & Todd.

Leboyer, F. (1975/2011). *Birth without Violence.* London: Pinter & Martin.

References

Levend, H., & Janus, L. (2000). *Drum hab ich kein Gesicht. Kinder aus unerwünschten Schwangerschaften.* Berlin: Echter.

Levine, P.A., & Frederick, A. (1997). *Walking the tiger: Healing trauma.* Berkeley: North Atlantic Books.

Liedloff, J. (1986). *The Continuum Concept: In Search of Happiness Lost.* Boston, MA: Da Capo Press.

Lipton, B.H. (2005). *The Biology of Belief: Unleashing the Power of Consciousness, Matter and Miracles.* Santa Rosa, CA: Mountain of Love.

Lipton, B.H. (2014). *The Honeymoon Effect: The Science of Creating Heaven on Earth.* Carlsbad, CA: Hay House.

Longfellow, H.W. (1847/1967). *Poems of Henry Wadsworth Longfellow.* The Crowell Poets. New York: Thomas Crowell.

Maher, M.S., Pine, F., & Bergman, A. (1975). *The Psychological Birth of the Human Infant: Symbiosis and Individuation.* New York: Basic Books.

Masters, A. (1981). *Nancy Astor, a biography.* New York: McGraw-Hill.

McQueen, T. (2013). What no one is talking about: Maternal death, mental, and physical trauma in the U.S. *Huffington Post, November.*

Merikangas, K.R., He, J., Surstein, M., Swanson, S.A., Avenevoli, S., Cui, L., … Swendsen, J. (2010). Lifetime prevalence of mental disorders in U.S. adolescents: Results from the national comorbidity study. *Journal of American Academy of Child and Adolescent Psychiatry, 49*(10), 980-989.

Middleton, D. (2009). A chiropractic look at germ theory. *Wellness Life Style, 23.*

Miller, A., & Hannum, H. (1985). *For your own good: Hidden cruelty in child-rearing and the roots of violence.* New York: Farrar, Straus and Giroux.

Montagu, A. (1962). *Prenatal influence.* Springfield, IL: Charles C. Thomas.

Montagu, A. (1978). *Touching: The Human Significance of Skin.* New York: Harper & Row.

Montagu, A. (1989). *Growing Young.* 2nd ed. Westport, CT: Greenwood Publishing Group, 1989.

Perry, B., & Szalavitz, M. (2007) *The Boy Who was raised as a dog: And other stories from a child psychiatrist's notebook—what traumatized children can teach us about loss, love, and healing.* New York: Basic Books.

References

Pert, C.B. (1999). *Molecules of Emotion: The science behind mind-body medicine.* New York: Simon & Schuster.

Prescott, J.W. (1975). *Brain function & malnutrition: Neuropsychological methods of assessment.* New York: John Wiley & Sons Publishing.

Raffi, A.R., Rondine, M., Grandi, S., & Fava, G.A. (2000). Life events and prodromal symptoms in bulimia nervosa. *Psychological Medicine, 30*(3), 727-731.

Robeznicks, A. (2015). US has highest maternal death rate among developed countries. *Modern Healthcare, May 6.*

Saint Exupery, A. de. (1943). *The Little Prince.* Translated by Katherine Woods. New York: Reynal & Hitchcock.

Secrest, M. (1998). *Frank Lloyd Wright: A Biography.* Chicago: University of Chicago Press.

Seligman, M. (1991). *Learned Optimism: How to change your mind and your life.* New York: Random House, p. 44-51.

Szejer, M. (2003). *Talking to babies: Healing with words on a maternity ward.* Boston: Beacon Press.

Szejer, M. (n.d.) Unpublished interview with Barbara Findeisen. Paris, France.

Tomatis, A.A. (1988/2005). *The ear and the voice.* Oxford: The Scarecrow Press, Inc.

Van de Bergh, B.R., & Marcoen, A. (2004). High antenatal maternal anxiety is related to ADHD symptoms, externalizing problems, and anxiety in 8- and 9-year-olds. *Child Development, 75*(4), 1085-1097.

van der Kolk, B. (2014). *The body keeps the score: Brain, mind, and body in the healing of trauma.* 1st ed. New York: Viking.

Verny, T.R., & Weintraub, P. (2002). *Tomorrow's baby: The art and science of parenting from conception through infancy.* New York: Simon & Schuster.

Verny, T.R., & Weintraub, P. (2003). *Pre-Parenting: Nurturing Your Child from Conception.* New York: Simon & Schuster.

Verny, T.R., & Kelly, J. (1981). *The Secret Life of the Unborn Child.* 1st ed. New York: Simon & Schuster.

References

Winnicott, D.W. (1992). *Psycho-analytic explorations*. Edited by Clare Winnicott and Ray Shepherd. Cambridge, MA: Harvard University Press.

Witt, A. (2015). Interview with Christopher Ingraham of the Washington Post on Weekends with Alex Witt, *MSNBC*, October 18.

Wordsworth, W. (1807/1967). *Poems in Two Volumes*. London: Longman, Hurst, Rees, and Orme.

World Health Organization. (2014). Trends in maternal mortality, 1990-2013. Retrieved from: http://www.who.int/reproductivehealth/publications/monitoring/maternal-mortality-2013/en/

Wright, F. L. (1943). *Frank Lloyd Wright: An Autobiography*. 3rd ed. New York: Duell, Sloan & Pearce.

CPSIA information can be obtained
at www.ICGtesting.com
Printed in the USA
FSHW011942281019
63509FS